Dinosaurs

For Thomas Atlay James

L. B. Halstead
Jenny Halstead

Dinosaurs

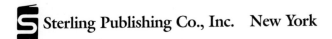
Sterling Publishing Co., Inc.   New York

Library of Congress Cataloging-in-Publication Data
Halstead, L. B.
  Dinosaurs.
  Originally published: Poole, Dorset : Blandford Press,
1981. (Blandford colour series)
  Includes index.
  1. Dinosaurs. I. Halstead, Jenny. II. Title.
QE862.D5H23   1987   567.9'1   87–15142
ISBN 0-8069-6626-2 (pbk.)

3   5   7   9   10   8   6   4   2

Published in 1987 by Sterling Publishing Co., Inc.
Two Park Avenue, New York, N.Y. 10016
First published in the U.K. by Blandford Press, Dorset
Copyright © 1981 by Blandford Books Ltd.
Distributed in Canada by Oak Tree Press Ltd.
% Canadian Manda Group, P.O. Box 920, Station U
Toronto, Ontario, Canada M8Z 5P9
Distributed in the United Kingdom by Blandford Press
Link House, West Street, Poole, Dorset BH15 1LL, England
Distributed in Australia by Capricorn Ltd.
P.O. Box 665, Lane Cove, NSW 2066
All rights reserved

Set in Monophoto Apollo by
Asco Trade Typesetting Ltd., Hong Kong.
Printed and bound in Hong Kong by
South China Printing Co.

Contents

Preface

Dinosaurs dominated the Earth for 140 million years and this book provides the most comprehensive survey of these ruling reptiles. *Dinosaurs* will serve as an encyclopaedia of dinosaurs to be used as a reference source for anyone with an interest in these animals. The first chapters give an account of the early discovery of dinosaur remains and then go on to discuss their origin and evolution. This introduction summarises the latest results of research into the behaviour and physiology of dinosaurs.

The colour section illustrates all the major types of dinosaur including many that have never previously figured in books, especially the recent discoveries made in China. Special attention has been paid to showing the probable colour patterns that the dinosaurs exhibited in life. Although the exact details of colour cannot be known with certainty, it is possible to work out the likely coloration and patterning by using modern analogues.

One of the important features of the illustrations is that on each double page all the species are shown to the same scale. A metre scale is included on each spread. As the aim of the book is to provide accurate details of the different dinosaurs, they are shown as isolated individuals in life positions. There has been no attempt at reconstructing environments or of showing them in landscapes. There are no restorations of interactions among the different kinds of dinosaur; such imaginative restorations are readily available in the numerous other popular dinosaur books. The bulk of the book provides a detailed classification of the dinosaurs with introductory paragraphs of all the major groups: two orders, six suborders and 32 different families. Over a hundred representative genera are described and illustrated. For every main group a detailed drawing of a skull is given and in a few instances complete well preserved skeletons are shown.

As well as the accurate figuring of all the main types of dinosaur, there are colour photographs of excavations as well as mounted skeletons, and such kinds of fossil as skin impressions, footprints and eggshells.

The book closes with a critical review of the various theories that have been put forward to account for their extinction 64 million years ago.

Dinosaurs is intended to be the major reference work on the different kinds of dinosaur that are known. Discoveries, particularly those made during the 1970s and in 1980, have been incorporated. Much of the material in this book and the restorations are based on the examination of dinosaur remains in many museums in the world, including those in Berlin, Chicago, London, Moscow, Paris, Peking, Tübingen and Washington, together with experiences on expeditions collecting fossil reptiles, especially in Africa.

L. B. H. & J. A. H. 1980

Acknowledgements

Grateful thanks are due to Professor Zofia Kielan-Jaworowska of the Polish Academy of Sciences in Warsaw and Dr Sun Ai-Lin and Dr Dong Zhi-Ming of the Institute of Vertebrate Palaeontology and Palaeoanthropology in Peking for their assistance and provision of illustrative material. Mr Cyril Walker provided photograph IX, Dr P. Taquet the photograph on page 15, and Mr J. Watkins photographs VII, X and XI. Thanks are due to Mr A. Cross for figures on pages 18, 21 24, 26, 27, 30, 35 and 60, to Mrs Irene Gillett who typed the manuscript and Mrs Anne Hardy for compiling the index.

1
The Discovery of Dinosaurs

The dinosaurs ruled the earth for the astonishing length of time of 140 million years. In spite of this monumental achievement they have acquired the reputation of being failures simply because they are no longer around. Their extinction is taken as a warning lesson of the dire consequences, firstly, of being too large and, secondly and more importantly, of the inability to adapt to changing circumstances. This dismissal of the dinosaurs is quite unfair. No-one rates Shakespeare a failure because he is no longer alive; he is recognised by what he left behind, just as are many of the great civilisations of the past. So it should be with the dinosaurs. They in their turn have left abundant evidence of themselves, monuments of their life and times.

The main evidence on which our knowledge of the dinosaurs is based comprises their fossilised bones and teeth. The first dinosaur bone ever described was the end of a femur or thigh bone found near Oxford which was described and illustrated by Robert Plot, the first keeper of the Ashmolean Museum in Oxford, in his book *The Natural History of Oxfordshire* published in 1677. Plot recognised that it was 'a real bone now petrified' and concluded that it 'must have belonged to some greater animal than either an ox or horse'. He discussed at length whether it could have come from an elephant brought over by the Romans but eventually concluded that it must have come from a giant man. Plot's successor at the Ashmolean, Edward Lhuyd, in his book *Lithophylaci Britannici Ichnographica* published a drawing of the tooth of a flesheating dinosaur in 1699. A further limb bone from Oxfordshire was described in 1758 by Joshua Platt, and in 1763 Richard Brookes published *The Natural History of Waters, Earths, Stones, Fossils, and Minerals; with their Virtues, Properties, and Medicinal Use. To which is added, The Method in which Linnaeus has treated these Subjects.* In this book the author republished Plot's original description and a copy, albeit reversed, of the bone in question. He labelled it *Scrotum humanum*. Since this was the first publication after 1758, the offically accepted beginning of zoological nomenclature, then *Scrotum humanum* was the first valid scientific name ever given to a dinosaur. The name was derived from the appearance of the articulating condyles at the knee-end of the bone. As this name was not used subsequently in the same context, under the International Rules of Zoological Nomenclature, the name is taken to have been forgotten and hence has ceased to be valid for dinosaurs.

It was not until the end of the eighteenth century that evidence began to accumulate that many large fossilised bones belonged to giant animals that no longer lived on the earth, that contrary to previous beliefs certain animals had become extinct before the arrival of man – a disconcerting notion to the ecclesiastical authorities of the time. During the early 1800s further bones were collected from near Oxford including part of a jawbone with large serrated blade-like teeth. These came into the possession of William Buckland, the first Professor of Geology at the University of Oxford. Many of his friends and colleagues viewed this material, which was recognised as belonging to a giant reptile. James Parkinson, now best known for having first described the symptoms of the shaking palsy known as Parkinson's disease, published a drawing of a tooth which he named *Megalosaurus* or 'great reptile' and suggested that in life it must have attained a length of 40 feet and stood 8 feet high. In metric terms such an animal would have been about 12m long and 2.5m high. His book *Outlines of Oryctology, an Introduction to the Study of Fossil Organic Remains* was published in July 1822.

Early in the same year a further discovery was made, this time in Sussex. A local medical doctor Gideon Mantell was visiting a patient near Cuckfield. He was an enthusiastic fossil collector and was completing his book *The Fossils of the South Downs, or Illustrations of the Geology of Sussex* illustrated by his wife. While Mantell was attending to his patient, his wife wandered down a track and came across a number of fossilised teeth embedded in pieces of Tilgate Stone, which was being used as road metal. These remains were recognised by Mantell as having belonged to some kind of giant plant-eating animal but although he realised their importance he was very hesitant about jumping to conclusions. Nevertheless, he included illustrations of them in his book, which was published in May 1822. He exhibited the teeth at the Geological Society of London and colleagues suggested they might be fish teeth or simply modern mammalian remains. Charles Lyell took a specimen to Paris to Georges Cuvier, the world's greatest expert on comparative anatomy and fossil vertebrates, who simply dismissed it as the upper incisor tooth of a rhinoceros. Meanwhile Mantell had located the quarry from which the remains had come and, as well as further teeth, he found a small

9

conical bone and some foot bones. These latter were identified as hippopotamus remains by Cuvier. Mantell was still not satisfied and in spite of these authoritative pronouncements continued his investigations. At the Royal College of Surgeons he had his attention drawn to the *Iguana* lizard from the Americas which had similar teeth but on a miniature scale. Mantell was now convinced that he had evidence of the former existence of a giant plant-eating lizard which he named *Iguanodon* or '*Iguana* tooth' and he presented his interpretation to the Royal Society of London in 1825. Meanwhile, following urgent requests from Cuvier, Buckland had published his description of *Megalosaurus* in 1824. The recognition of the former existence of giant plant-eating and flesh-eating reptiles, which had never been suspected, together with curious marine reptiles and flying reptiles, captured the public imagination, notwithstanding the denunciations that such discoveries elicited from the pulpit. Here was incontrovertible evidence that the Book of Genesis could no longer be accepted as the literal account of creation.

In spite of the wondrous nature of these giant reptiles, they were simply scaled up versions of modern lizards. It was not until 1841, when Richard Owen in his Report on British Fossil Reptiles presented to the meeting of the British Association for the Advancement of Science, that the concept of the dinosaur was first introduced to the public. Owen showed that it was not possible simply to scale up fossil reptiles on the basis of living forms as that would have produced 60m (200ft) long lizards. From his study of the vertebrae and limb bones he was able to establish beyond any shadow of doubt that these animals, for which he coined the name Dinosauria, held their limbs beneath their bodies in exactly the same way as mammals, that they were the reptilian equivalents of the pachyderms – the rhinoceroses, elephants and hippopotamuses. Owen stressed the fact that the dinosaurs were the peak of the reptilian creation and since their day the history of the reptiles had been one of degeneration rather than progressive evolution. Owen then produced restorations of *Iguanodon* and *Megalosaurus* on the basis of his interpretations. Lifesize concrete models were built by Waterhouse Hawkins under Owen's direction and set up in south London in the Crystal Palace park at Sydenham where they still stand in their primaeval glory.

The European monopoly of dinosaur discoveries was broken in the 1850s when Joseph Leidy described a skeleton excavated by W. P. Foulke which he named *Hadrosaurus foulkii*. Contrary to all expectations the length of the fore and hind limbs were very different. Leidy considered that *Hadrosaurus* must have stood in the manner of

Statues of Iguanodon *built by Waterhouse Hawkins in 1854, in the Crystal Palace Gardens, South London.*

a kangaroo propped up on its tail. Later Edward Drinker Cope discovered a leaping flesh-eater, a relative of *Megalosaurus*, in which the forelimbs were so small that they were unlikely to have been of much use at all in locomotion. In 1878 miners at Bernissart, Belgium, while following a coal seam suddenly ran into sands containing masses of bones of over thirty complete skeletons of *Iguanodon*, eleven mounted skeletons of which are now on display in the Royal Museum of Natural History, Brussels. This dramatic discovery finally settled for all time that *Iguanodon* stood and walked on its hind limbs and that the structure that was thought to be a nasal horn was in fact a specialised thumb spike.

It was during the last three decades of the nineteenth century that the world's greatest collections of dinosaurs were amassed as a result of the tremendous exertions of Cope and Othniel Charles Marsh, both dedicated fossil hunters and deeply antagonistic towards one another. Each was determined to be first in discovering and naming new types of dinosaur. They were not above planting spies in one another's camps, buying off one another's collectors and even diverting train-loads of bones; the ruthless drive for bones and the obvious hatred fought out on occasion in the pages of the popular press resulted in

11

the largest collections of dinosaur bones ever made. Such bitter rivalry spurred both men on to heights neither would have achieved without the incentive to keep ahead of the enemy. Marsh was slow and painstaking in his work in contrast to the brilliant and prolific Cope who published over 1400 papers, books and monographs. Both men were of independent means and their entire fortunes were spent on financing their collecting.

By the turn of the century both Cope and Marsh had died and by then several major institutions with financial backing from such millionaires as the steel magnate Andrew Carnegie were excavating complete skeletons and mounted skeletons were beginning to adorn some of the world's major museums – perhaps the most famous being that of *Diplodocus*. The resources required for the full-scale excavation of complete dinosaur skeletons were enormous. Immediately prior to World War 1 the German expeditions to East Africa from 1909 to 1912 were financed by a public fund set up in 1907 which collected the equivalent of 50,000 dollars. The prize of the German collecting is seen in the mounted skeleton of *Brachiosaurus* in Berlin. The Central Asiatic Expeditions from the American Museum of Natural History in the 1920s are reputed to have cost up to a million dollars. The only really large scale dinosaur expeditions since then have been those to Mongolia organised by the Russians in the 1950s and the joint Polish-Mongolian ones in the late 1960s and early 1970s. During the last thirty years, there has been a slow but steady collection of dinosaurs in China, which are on display in several Chinese museums.

Hunting for dinosaurs today

There are still many parts of the world where dinosaurs await discovery, but in order to collect them several years of planning are usually required. By far the most important aspect is making a detailed case to solicit financial support. It is necessary to have run a preliminary reconnaissance so that the logistics for the full scale expedition can be planned in depth. On the evidence obtained from such preliminary expeditions, it is then possible to present a very detailed programme, which will generally obtain the necessary financial backing. In the 1980s this type of preparation is not enough. Most new sites are in difficult terrain, in remote regions of the globe, in the hinterland of newly independent countries which often tend to be suspicious of international teams wandering around their territory. The major effort in planning an expedition becomes a political exercise involving long drawn out negotiations especially with regard to the final destination of the specimens. In view of the national

Mounted skeleton of Brachiosaurus *in the Palaeontological Museum of Humboldt University, Berlin.*

prestige that a country stands to acquire from having their own mounted dinosaurs, it is normal practice nowadays for the main collections to be returned to the host country after the necessary research has been completed. Even when all these problems have been overcome such expeditions are not without their hazards. The association of fossil collecting with geology and mineral resources can easily lead sensitive authorities to treat dinosaur hunters with suspicion. Expeditions can suddenly, for no apparent reason, find themselves apprehended and this is by no means a rare occurrence especially if the fossiliferous sites are close to international frontiers. Such indeed was the experience of the International Palaeontological Expedition to Sokoto State, Nigeria, in the winter of 1977–78. In this instance the matter was eventually resolved by the personal intervention of Sokoto State's Military Governor, the late Brigadier Umaru Alhaji Mohammed.

Once all the local problems are resolved, the actual expedition can get underway. Such expeditions have to be entirely self-sufficient while in the field and by far the most vital commodity is water. The best preserved material seems invariably to be found in hot desert regions. Four-wheel drive vehicles modified for travel in exceedingly rough terrain are absolutely essential, including lorries for the transport of the specimens. Picks, shovels, hammers, chisels for exposing the materials, plaster of Paris and old newspapers, toilet paper and burlap strips for protecting the specimens and wood for making crates to pack them in.

One of the major problems that was discovered during the great dinosaur bone rush in the United States was that, after wagon loads of brittle fossilised bones had been driven across hundreds of miles of rough terrain, it was not unusual for the bones to have been reduced to piles of useless rubble. The basic technique by which this problem is overcome is attributed to Cope. He was aware from his own experience of the dire need to protect the specimens from the inevitable deterioration during the long haul back to the museum. Simply wrapping them was not sufficient. It so happened that the major provisions for any trek into the Wild West in the 1870s were sacks of rice. This was a food stuff of which Cope was not at all fond and hence there was an excess of it. This was boiled up and strips of the sacking were soaked in the resulting paste and then bandaged over the specimens. On drying out the paste hardened to form a protective jacket around the precious specimens. Subsequently plaster of Paris was used but the basic technique has remained unchanged.

When dinosaur bones are located they are carefully exposed by carefully chiselling away the enclosing rock. The bones have numbers painted on them and a detailed and accurate plan is made of all the skeletal remains as a record of exactly how they were found. Such plans are especially important when it comes to analysing the conditions in which the animals came to be preserved. The individual

Dinosaur backbone exposed in the Sahara Desert in Niger.

bones are coated with damp tissue and then strips of sacking dipped in plaster of Paris bandage the bones and then a thick plaster cast is made encasing the exposed part of the bone. Once this has been accomplished the rock underneath the bone is excavated so that the specimen is supported on a kind of rocky pedestal. The supports are carefully severed and the block turned over. The entire specimen is then encased in plaster and the jacket numbered and packed in wooden crates to be loaded onto the lorry for transport to railhead or port for shipment back to the Museum or Research Institute.

Once the material is safely back in the laboratory the plaster jackets are carefully removed and the bone is diligently freed from the enclosing rock. It is the practice nowadays to make lightweight fibreglass casts of the individual bones, so that the complete skeleton can be assembled in a life-like pose with the minimum of engineering support problems.

In some circumstances it may be decided to put the bones on display in exactly the position in which they were preserved. In such a situation the original field plan of the bones serves as the blueprint for arranging the bones once they have been removed from their plaster jackets.

15

The fossil evidence

The main evidence on which knowledge of dinosaurs is based is that of their preserved bones and teeth. It is from the skeletons that the overall shape and posture of dinosaurs can be accurately determined. From the proportions of the bones and muscle scars it is possible to reconstruct the muscles of dinosaurs and work out the type of movements that were possible. The construction of the limbs and limb girdles is evidence of posture but fossil footprints provide proof of the exact way the dinosaurs strode the earth. The evidence of trackways not only confirmed that their gait was basically mammalian as Owen had recognised but it has even allowed the speed at which the individuals were moving to be calculated.

An examination of the different types of dentition generally gives a clear indication of the diet of the dinosaur concerned. Worn flattened teeth or blunt peg-like teeth indicate a herbivorous diet, whereas sharp serrated blade-like teeth are equally indicative of flesh-eating. Such conclusions occasionally receive dramatic confirmation from the actual preservation of stomach contents. In the case of the skeleton of the tiny *Compsognathus* a small lizard is preserved in its stomach and duckbilled dinosaur remains are known with pine needles and cones in their stomachs. The presence of highly polished pebbles, stomach stones or gastroliths, used for breaking up food, reveal important information about the digestive processes of dinosaurs. It can be assumed that these functioned exactly as they do in crocodiles by pounding up food.

The texture of the skin of dinosaurs is well known in those forms that possessed a bony armour but there are numerous examples of mummified remains where the animals died in desert conditions and the sediment preserved the fine details of skin texture. There are occasional examples of skin impressions being left where a dinosaur has sat on damp sands. The other type of dinosaur fossil that is important in reconstructing their way of life are the remains of dinosaur eggs. In the case of eggshells, bones and teeth it is possible to study their microscopic structure by making thin sections.

It is from a combination of these different types of fossil that the way of life of the dinosaurs can be reconstructed with a reasonable degree of accuracy. At the same time, in order to provide a clear understanding of the environment in which they lived, it is also necessary to study the rocks in which the remains are preserved. These provide direct evidence of the environment in which the remains were preserved and it is generally possible to infer from this the conditions in which they actually lived.

2
Origin and Evolution of Dinosaurs

The ancestry of the dinosaurs can be traced back to small lizard-like reptiles inhabiting the extensive tropical Carboniferous coal swamps of about 300 million years ago and feeding on the abundant insect life. Most of the vertebrates inhabiting the swamps were semiaquatic, feeding on fish and other aquatic organisms so that their teeth and jaws acted essentially as fish traps and the function of the teeth was simply to prevent the prey from slipping out and escaping. The more terrestrial members of the community had to be able to hold their prey firmly as it struggled and had also to be able to dispatch it. The sloping bone at the back of the skull on which the lower jaw articulated – the quadrate – swung forwards so that it was oriented in a vertical plane hence making the jaw a more efficient and stronger mechanism. One of the main problems in improving the jaw apparatus was the need to be able to increase the jaw musculature. In all primitive reptiles the jaw muscles are situated between the braincase and the temporal or cheek bones and the space is thus rigidly confined. However, there were two places where three bones met and during evolution the developing muscles prevented these triple junctions from uniting, so that two temporal openings formed, allowing extra muscle development to take place. The first reptile to develop this double opening was *Petrolacosaurus* from the Upper Carboniferous. This reptile represents the beginning of two major evolutionary lineages: the lepidosaurs leading to the lizards and snakes, and the archosaurs which include the crocodiles and dinosaurs. The feature which characterised the archosaurs was the formation of a further opening on the side of the head, the preorbital fenestra, which was a rather basin-shaped depression and most probably housed a salt gland, a specialised organ for excreting excess salt. This feature probably enabled these early archosaurs to live in desert conditions.

The fundamental feature of the reptiles which distinguishes them from their amphibian contemporaries was their method of reproduction. Whereas the amphibians laid their eggs in water and spent the

Geological time scale and family tree of dinosaurs. The age at the beginning of each period is given in millions of years.

early part of their life history as gill-breathing tadpoles, the reptiles laid a shelled egg on land. Instead of the parents having to produce large numbers of eggs, the reptilian strategy was to lay only a few, each with the embryo enclosed in its own private pond enclosed in a membrane – the amnion. A further membrane – the allantois – acted as a respiratory and excretory organ, and the embryo was also provided with a food store – the yolk. Finally, the entire system was enclosed in a protective membrane, the chorion, which became impregnated with calcium carbonate.

With the drying up of the coal swamps, the animals with the amniote or cleidoic (closed) egg were able to reproduce without being forced to seek open bodies of water for their developing offspring. They were able to achieve the conquest of dry land.

The first reptiles that colonised the continents were not in any way related to the dinosaurs, they were the paramammals or mammal-like reptiles and they dominated the Earth for some 70 million years. They gradually became more mammalian until eventually several forms crossed the arbitrary barrier erected by palaeontologists between reptiles and mammals and became true mammals. During this Age of Paramammals, the ancestors of the lizards and archosaurs remained small insect-eating animals occupying an ecological niche close to the base of the food chain.

By the beginning of the Triassic period, some 225 million years ago, the archosaurs entered an ecological niche that had never been colonised by the paramammals. They became semiaquatic feeders and scavengers, filling the role of the present day crocodiles. The main changes that took place among these early archosaurs were concerned with rendering these reptiles better fitted for this particular way of life. The long tail became flattened from side to side and exceedingly powerful; this was the main propulsive organ which drove the animals through the water. At the same time the hind limbs which provided the initial thrust from a stationary position became longer and stronger than the forelimbs. Both for swimming and providing the initial push, the limbs would be more effective if the main movement were from the shoulder and hip joints so that the entire length of the limbs could be used. The basic reptilian method of moving is a sprawling gait, indeed the name reptile itself comes from the Latin verb *repere*, to crawl or to creep. The upper arm, or humerus, and thigh, or femur, are held out sideways and the main stride is from the elbow and knee. If the limbs are straightened and movement is from the shoulder and hips a longer and more effective stride becomes possible. This type of specialisation for a semiaquatic mode of life is again seen in living crocodiles, where the hind limbs are longer than the forelimbs and they can move at speed with the limbs held more or less straight, holding the body and tail well off the ground. This is the so-called 'high walk'. When such predators ventured onto land, the adaptations that had developed to improve their locomotion in the water became particularly important. With their upright posture, with the limbs held beneath the body, their effective stride was particularly long and this meant that they had the potential to move at considerable speed. However, in view of the marked difference in the lengths of the fore-limbs and hind-limbs, it meant that when moving on all four legs the maximum speed would have been determined by the shorter front legs. The speed capability of the hind limbs would have greatly exceeded that of the forelimbs. For an active predator, speed is especially important for capturing prey and the greatest speed would be achieved by the use of the hind limbs alone. With the body raised up off the ground and the fore-limbs lifted out of the way, the heavy muscular tail would act as a counterbalance, so that the entire body would have been pivoted about the hip girdle. It was the re-emergence of the archosaurs from the water that heralded the beginning of the Age of the Dinosaurs.

The first dinosaurs were bipedal flesh-eaters and their invasion of the land was responsible for the collapse of the Age of the Para-mammals. Very few paramammals survived beyond the end of the Triassic period, among the last being a small herbivorous form, *Oligokyphus*, which filled the ecological niche of modern water rats or voles. By this time, however, a few paramammals had crossed the mammalian threshold so that the beginning of the Age of Dinosaurs also witnessed the origin of the mammals which 140 million years later were to replace the dinosaurs as masters of the Earth.

The Triassic dinosaurs
The arrival towards the end of the Triassic period of active bipedal predators led to the collapse of the food chain that had evolved over the previous 70 million years. These, the first of the dinosaurs, were distinguished from their semiaquatic ancestors in the structure of their limbs and limb girdles, especially the hip girdle. This girdle was made up of three bones oriented in exactly the same way as in most reptiles and hence this division of the dinosaurs is known as saurischians or reptile-hipped. The main difference, however, was that the three bones did not form a solid bony wall at their junction but there was an open window or fenestra and the upper bone fused to the sacrum, the ilium, had developed a lateral bony shelf above the

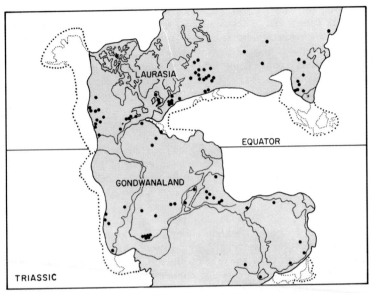

Palaeogeography of Triassic times, with dinosaur distribution (after C. B. Cox).

articulation to prevent the femur from slipping out of the joint. The femur had its articulating part developed at the side so that the leg was habitually held in an upright stance in contrast to normal reptiles where the femur sticks out sideways. Because the carnivorous dinosaurs walked on their hind limbs only and clearly walked in a mammalian manner, they were named theropods or beast-footed. There were two main kinds of these dinosaurs, a more heavily built form which still retained a bony armour in the skin, the carnosaurs or flesh reptiles, and the more lightly built type with light hollow bones, the coelurosaurs or hollow-reptiles. The lightly built kinds had long necks and tails and comparatively small skulls.

From an analysis of footprints, it is evident that the carnivorous dinosaurs moved around in groups and it is inferred from this that they hunted in packs. The carnosaurs usually walked at 4.5kph (2¾mph) but when closing in for a kill could reach 8kph (5mph). In contrast the coelurosaurs had a normal walking speed of 8kph (5mph) and were capable of running up to 13kph (8mph).

During the late Triassic a further saurischian group of dinosaurs made its appearance. These had long necks and tails and small heads and in this respect were similar to the coelurosaurs to which they were more closely related than to the carnosaurs. However, they had more massively constructed limbs and bodies and generally seem to have walked on all fours. Their teeth were similar to those of the carnivorous dinosaurs although much smaller. These four-footed early dinosaurs are known as prosauropods which means first reptile-footed, in contrast to the beast-footed theropods. The prosauropods are important as they represent the first group of dinosaurs to become plant-eaters. This group is notable for the tremendous increase in size from 2m long to the largest reaching a length of 12m (6½ft to 40ft). This increase in size is a further indication of their change in food preferences, and increase in bulk would have provided a measure of protection.

Towards the end of the Triassic period a number of small 1m long dinosaurs are known, which superficially looked like the small bipedal carnivores. However, they differed fundamentally in two important features. In the hip girdle the anterior bone, the pubis, instead of pointing forwards was aligned alongside and parallel to the posterior bone, the ischium. This arrangement is found today only in birds and for this reason such dinosaurs are known as ornithischians or bird-hipped reptiles. There is a further feature, which is the trademark of this group, and that is the possession of a single bone at the tip of the lower jaw just in front of the tooth-bearing bone, the dentary, and because it is in front it is called the predentary bone. From the teeth it is evident that these dinosaurs were exclusively plant-eaters. It is not known how they are related to the saurischian dinosaurs and it is believed that they represent a separate evolutionary lineage from a group of semiaquatic herbivorous archosaurs. The upright bipedal posture is likely to have arisen in the same way as it did with the carnivores, as an adaptation to a semiaquatic mode of life. A plant-eater inhabiting the same environment as flesh-eaters needs to be able to move as swiftly as the predators if it is to stand much chance of survival.

The Triassic period is notable for the extensive desert areas in the world and marked seasonal droughts. The small ornithischians are known to have aestivated, that is, to have slept during the dry season, in the same way that reptiles and mammals in temperate latitudes today sleep during the winter. In the tropics today crocodiles also sleep during the dry season.

The Triassic period witnessed the origin of the dinosaurs and the establishment of the main evolutionary lineages that were to develop dramatically in the succeeding geological periods. The Triassic set the scene for the Age of Dinosaurs.

The Jurassic dinosaurs

During the Jurassic period – 190 to 136 million years ago – the major dinosaur groups already established in the Triassic experienced important evolutionary developments. The increase in size which the prosauropods had begun was carried to indescribable lengths with the sauropods. *Diplodocus* reached a length of 28m (90ft) with its enormously long neck and whip-like tail but in life weighed only 10 tonnes. *Apatosaurus*, formerly known as *Brontosaurus*, was shorter, 25m (80ft), but three times the weight, while the recently discovered 'Supersaurus' was about 30m (100ft) long and weighed up to 100 tonnes – as much as the giant whalebone whales of the modern oceans. Amazingly these greatest giants the Earth has ever supported lived in herds. Furthermore, when they were on the move the smaller individuals and more vulnerable members of the group walked in the centre of the group and the larger ones at the perimeter. These huge reptiles walked at between 3 and 4kph ($2-2\frac{1}{2}$mph). The advantage of such huge sizes was that their internal temperature must have remained constant – in other words, these dinosaurs were homoiothermic. Whereas birds and mammals maintain a constant internal temperature by burning up large amounts of food – that is, they have a high metabolic rate – the dinosaurs achieved the same end result simply by being large. It has been calculated that with an air temperature daily fluctuating between 22° and 32°C for a reptile with a diameter of 1m, the daily temperature fluctuation in the body would have been between 28.5° and 29.5°C. The one major problem to which such dinosaurs would have been susceptible, however, would have been excess heat. The elongated tails and necks would have increased the surface area and could have acted as cooling mechanisms. The one area that would have been particularly vulnerable to overheating would have been the head and brain and it would have been essential to keep the brain cool as it was situated close to the surface, and the skin temperature would have fluctuated almost as much as the air temperatures. The dinosaurs developed extensive nasal passages and the membranes would have provided an important evaporative cooling surface. There is evidence in some dinosaurs of large venous sinuses near the brain, which would also have acted as a heat control mechanism. From the structure of the sauropods, it is evident that they must have had the basic low metabolism of reptiles

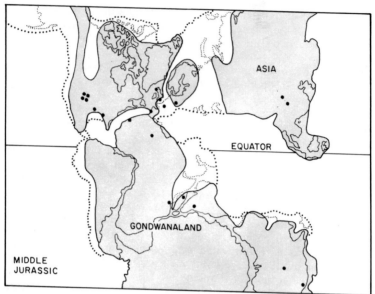

Palaeogeography of Jurassic times, with dinosaur distribution (after C. B. Cox).

and in no way whatsoever could they have had a high metabolic rate in the same sense as mammals. It would have been physically impossible for them to have ingested sufficient food in any 24 hours to fuel themselves for life at a high metabolic rate. It seems by far the most probable that they spent a large proportion of their time in the waters of lakes and swamps raking plants with their peg-like teeth (some such as *Diplodocus* only had teeth at the front of the skull). These dinosaurs were capable of swimming as footprint trackways are known of front feet only, proving that they floated in the water with just their front feet pawing the bottom, in the manner of swimming hippopotamuses.

As well as the sauropods, the heavily built carnosaurs similarly evolved large forms such as *Allosaurus* with a length of 11m (36ft) and a capability of walking at up to 8kph (5mph), double the speed of the giant herbivores. It was assumed that the herbivores could always escape by retreating into the deeper waters where the flesh-eaters could not reach them. However, in 1980, trackways of swimming carnosaurs were recorded for the first time. In fact considering the semiaquatic ancestry of the carnosaurs, it would have been surprising if they had lost their swimming ability entirely. These recent discoveries have proved that this ability had indeed been retained. In complete contrast the coelurosaurs seem to have evolved extremely small forms such as the 600mm (2ft) long *Compsognathus*, which hunted lizards, as is evidenced by its stomach contents. The significance of these tiny coelurosaurs is that in many details of their skeleton they were remarkably similar to the first bird *Archaeopteryx* which can be thought of as a small dinosaur invested with feathers. It is from the detailed study of the coelurosaur skeleton that many scientists have concluded that the dinosaurs did not completely die out, but are represented in the modern world by their direct descendants – birds.

The herbivorous ornithischians illustrate similar trends to those of the carnivorous dinosaurs. From the small Triassic bipedal forms, there evolved two major lineages. The main line was simply a continuation of the small lightly built types but in the second lineage there was a progressive increase in size to give such forms as *Camptosaurus* and *Iguanodon*. The ornithischians all developed a number of remarkable specialisations for a plant-eating way of life, which were unique among reptiles. As Mantell recognised from the moment his wife showed him the teeth of *Iguanodon* in 1822, these reptiles wore down their teeth – this means they must have been capable of grinding or chewing their food. From a study of the skulls, it can be shown that they possessed muscular cheeks, otherwise known only among mammals. They even developed a secondary palate, so that their food and air passages could be kept separate. This enabled them to retain food in the mouth to chew it and breathe at the same time. This condition parallels the situation in the mammals to a remarkable degree and is one of the most dramatic examples in the fossil record of convergent evolution – two entirely separate lines evolving similar structures to subserve similar functions. The bipedal ornithischians are grouped together as ornithopods or bird footed on account of their bird-like three toed feet.

From the beginning of the Jurassic, remains of a primitive armoured ornithischian *Scelidosaurus* are known. This form is a representative of the most primitive type of ornithischian, which is the least changed from their quadrupedal semiaquatic ancestors. There is not a great deal of difference between the lengths of the fore and hind-limbs and the primitive protective armour is still present. This is the first member of the ankylosaurs, or fused reptiles, and during the

Jurassic they gave rise to a further armoured group which bore large triangular plates or spines running along the length of the body. These were the stegosaurs or roofed reptiles.

The Jurassic fauna of large carnosaurs, small coelurosaurs, giant sauropods, large and small ornithopods and stegosaurs is found in North America, Europe, Asia and Africa. In fact there seem to have been land connections linking all the continents of the world so that the same basic type of dinosaurs was found everywhere, although there were important geographical variations.

The Cretaceous dinosaurs

During the early part of the Cretaceous period, beginning 136 million years ago, the dinosaur faunas of the world were not significantly different from those of the preceding Jurassic. During the latter part of the Cretaceous, in contrast, major changes began to take place. The continents drifted apart to such an extent that the dinosaurs were no longer able to move freely; they were isolated in different regions. By

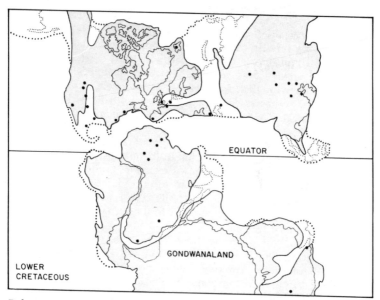

Palaeogeography of Lower Cretaceous times, with dinosaur distribution (after C. B. Cox).

far the most important change that occurred was in the plant life; modern flowering plants evolved in the northern continents. In the southern continents there were no striking changes and the dinosaurs do not seem to have changed in any significant way; the dinosaur faunas were essentially what they had been in the Jurassic period. In the northern continents it was an entirely different story. In the single continent that encompassed western North America and eastern Asia, the dinosaurs experienced their most dramatic evolutionary radiation.

The carnosaurs reached their culmination in the giant *Tyrannosaurus*, the largest flesh-eater of all time, reaching a length of 12m (40ft). In spite of its ferocious appearance *Tyrannosaurus* was a slow moving scavenger incapable of moving much faster than 4kph ($2\frac{1}{2}$mph). A single corpse of a 30 tonne sauropod would have provided enough food for a tyrannosaur individual for three years. Hence in the general economy of the time, such giant scavengers could be easily supported.

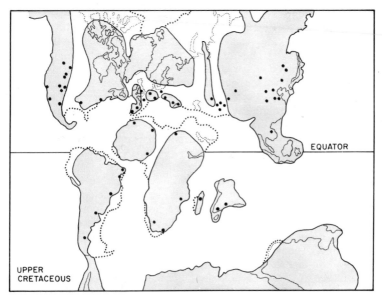

Palaeogeography of Upper Cretaceous times, with dinosaur distribution (after C. B. Cox).

By far the most dramatic evolutionary developments were among the descendants of the coelurosaurs. The most active flesh-eaters were the deinonychosaurs, the terrible-clawed reptiles, in which the second toe was developed into an enormous sickle-like slashing and ripping weapon. These 2–3m (6½–10ft) long dinosaurs were active pack hunters with a highly developed sense of balance and were specialised for leaping onto their prey. The other line that evolved from the coelurosaurs was that of the ornithomimosaurs or bird mimic reptiles, the so-called ostrich dinosaurs. These had lost their teeth and possessed a toothless beak. They had very long legs and long grasping fingers. It is thought that they preyed on dinosaur eggs and also hunted dinosaur hatchlings, as well as lizards and mammals. Some even evolved binocular vision. The most striking feature of these two groups was their brains. The size of the brain in relation to the body was far greater than in any other dinosaur or indeed any known living reptile. In fact their brain capacity was within the range of modern birds and close to that of mammals. The advanced brain of these dinosaurs was connected with their extremely advanced eyesight and highly developed sense of balance. In any event they were more highly evolved than any other type of reptile.

Among the herbivores of the time there were equally dramatic developments taking place. The sauropods continued without any noticeable change. The ankylosaurs, the heavily armoured ornithischians, evolved a variety of thick bony plates and protective spikes but the most sensational developments took place among the bipedal ornithopods. By far the most successful were the duck-billed dinosaurs or hadrosaurs which evolved from the larger heavily built ornithopods. These developed an enormous battery of grinding teeth for dealing with tough plant materials such as pine needles, but by far the most curious structures were the variously shaped crests on the top of the skull. These contained greatly expanded nasal passages and their interpretation has been a subject of considerable discussion. The latest theory is that they acted as resonating chambers for the dinosaurs to call to one another. It is known from footprints that the hadrosaurs lived in herds and also that they colonised a variety of habitats from cypress swamps and broadleaf woodland to open shrubland. The shapes of the head crests would have served as recognition signals in conjunction with appropriate calls. The hadrosaurs seems to have been among the most advanced and successful of all the herbivorous dinosaurs. Perhaps one of the most surprising discoveries recorded in 1979 was the evidence of hadrosaur nurseries. The parent dinosaurs had constructed a nest mound of mud 1.5m high and 3m across (5ft high and 10ft across) and with a saucer-like hollow 2m across and 0.75m deep ($6\frac{1}{2}$ft across and $2\frac{1}{2}$ft deep) excavated at the summit. In this depression were the skeletal remains of 11 young hadrosaurs up to 1m in length and all with worn teeth. This means that after hatching the young stayed together living in a nest site that must have been extremely conspicuous in the landscape – an open invitation to any passing predator. The only explanation for such an occurrence is that the site must have been under the protection of the adults. Presumably the young would have followed the parent while feeding and at night would have been protected by the proximity of the adults somewhat in the manner of, say, ostriches, although it is not possible to imagine the 3 tonne adults actually sitting on the nest.

The other evolutionary developments were from the lightly built ornithopods. One evolutionary lineage was characterised by the progressive thickening of the bone at the very summit of the skull culminating in *Pachycephalosaurus* with a 250mm (10in) thick roof to its skull. These pachycephalosaurs, thick headed reptiles or bone-heads, seem to have developed this thickening as reptilian battering rams and it is believed that they were used in ritual contests between competing males. It is inferred that there was a hierarchy within the herd as in some birds and also among some living reptiles, where there is a dominant male who achieves and maintains his position through such intraspecific contests. A similar situation has been postulated for the final dinosaur group to have evolved from the small lightly built ornithopods. From such lightly built forms as *Psittacosaurus* or parrot-reptile there evolved the heavily built quadrupedal ceratopsians or horned reptiles. These culminated in the huge three horned *Triceratops* with its large bony frill extending over the neck region. The ceratopsians evolved a large variety of kinds and the different types of bony frill and horns are thought to have been primarily display structures to both impress and intimidate rivals of the same species, again with the aim of establishing supremacy among the herd. There is direct evidence that the horns of *Triceratops* were used in such trials of strength between members of the same species, because some bony frills showed healed wounds that could only have been made by the horns of other individuals.

The evidence of the variety of display structures on the skulls of the hadrosaurs, the bone-heads and the ceratopsians, together with the nesting sites of both ceratopsians and hadrosaurs suggest that these most advanced of the plant-eating dinosaurs had evolved complex and relatively sophisticated social structures and behavioural

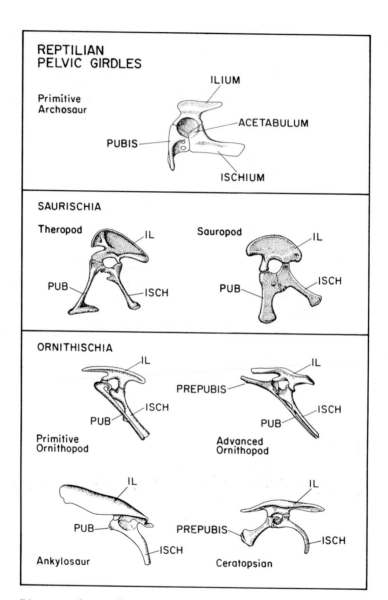

Dinosaur pelvic girdles.

patterns. This has led some authors to suggest that the dinosaurs were significantly more advanced than living reptiles and represented a grade of organisation in advance of reptiles, so that the dinosaurs should be separated from reptiles and grouped in a separate class of the vertebrates. It has even been suggested that their success was due to their having a high metabolic rate in the same sense as birds and mammals. It is, however, now generally recognised that the dinosaurs achieved a constant internal temperature simply by virtue of their small surface area compared to their volume, a passive homoiothermy. Furthermore, the behavioural patterns inferred for the dinosaurs can all be matched among living reptiles: crocodiles are known to build nests and protect them and even to guard their young which live in crocodile nurseries. The social structure and intraspecific contests are similarily observed among many tropical reptiles. In fact on all acounts the dinosaurs seem to have been by far the most advanced of all the reptiles, but reptiles nonetheless.

As Richard Owen correctly recognised, the dinosaurs represented the very peak of reptilian life.

3
Dinosaur Classification

There are over 800 different species of dinosaur so far known and further remains are being continually discovered. Many forms are only known from isolated bones which prove the existence of different species but do not provide sufficient evidence to allow a reconstruction of the complete skeleton to be made. Some species are distinguished on minor anatomical features of particular bones which would not be observable in life restorations. For this reason the descriptive section only deals with the dinosaurs for which adequate evidence is available to allow life restorations to be attempted.

Dinosaurs are distinguished from all other reptiles by the manner in which they stood and walked. Whereas living reptiles have a sprawling gait with the limbs more or less sticking out sideways from the body, in the dinosaurs the limbs were held vertically beneath. This difference in posture means that the stride of a dinosaur was from the shoulder and hip girdles and not as in lizards from the elbow and knee. In this respect dinosaur locomotion was more efficient than that of typical reptiles and indeed the dinosaurs owed much of their success to this improved method of moving around. In their posture and gait the dinosaurs were more akin to birds and mammals than typical reptiles. The dinosaurs represented the peak of reptilian evolution and this fundamental functional attribute of the dinosaurs is clearly reflected in the structure of their limbs and limb girdles. This is best seen in the pelvic girdle. As with all reptiles, as well as birds and mammals, the pelvic girdle consists of three elements: a dorsal ilium which is fused to the sacral vertebrae and, ventrally, an anterior pubic bone and posterior ischium. The upper limb bone, the femur, articulates at the region where these three pelvic bones meet. This articulating cup-shaped hollow is termed the acetabulum and in animals in which the limbs are habitually held out sideways the three-bone junction is floored by a bony wall made up of segments from each contributing bone of the girdle. In dinosaurs, with the limbs held vertically, there is no force exerted in this region and in consequence there is no longer a solid wall of bone but instead an open space or fenestra. In order that the limb will not slip out of the socket a bony shelf develops on the upper part of the articulation. Without it the upright posture of dinosaurs would hardly be possible. Any reptile with this type of limb girdle can be classified as a dinosaur. Indeed it was on just such characters that Richard Owen in 1841 introduced the name Dinosauria, a name which has been used ever since for such reptiles. Subsequent to Owen's recognition of this major group of extinct vertebrates, it was discovered that the dinosaurs fell into two contrasting groups on the basis of two quite distinct types of pelvic girdle. In one group the pubis pointed forwards as in most normal reptiles and this group was hence named Saurischia or reptile-hipped; in the second group the pubis pointed backwards to lie parallel to the ischium somewhat in the manner of the bird pelvis and hence such dinosaurs were grouped together in the Ornithischia or bird-hipped reptiles.

Table 1

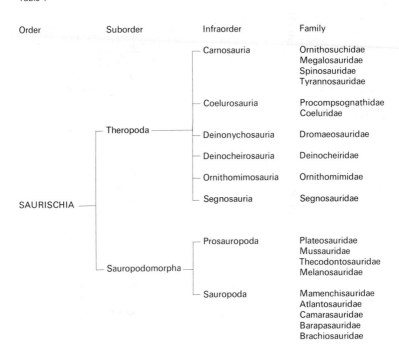

Order	Suborder	Infraorder	Family
		Carnosauria	Ornithosuchidae Megalosauridae Spinosauridae Tyrannosauridae
		Coelurosauria	Procompsognathidae Coeluridae
	Theropoda	Deinonychosauria	Dromaeosauridae
		Deinocheirosauria	Deinocheiridae
		Ornithomimosauria	Ornithomimidae
SAURISCHIA		Segnosauria	Segnosauridae
	Sauropodomorpha	Prosauropoda	Plateosauridae Mussauridae Thecodontosauridae Melanosauridae
		Sauropoda	Mamenchisauridae Atlantosauridae Camarasauridae Barapasauridae Brachiosauridae

Saurischia (Table 1)
The saurischian dinosaurs are characterised by their retention of the basic primitive type of pelvic girdle in which the three bones are arranged as in the normal reptiles with the ilium at the top, the pubis pointing forwards and the ischium backwards. The ilium is expanded into a forwards facing blade and its lower surface situated above the limb joint develops a strong bony shelf. The three bones do not form a solid bony plate in the region where they meet, as they do in more primitive reptiles, but instead there is an open space bounded by the three bones concerned. There are two fundamentally different types of saurischian – a more primitive group, the Theropoda, which comprised the flesh-eating dinosaurs and were exclusively bipedal, and the Sauropodomorpha, which were quadrupedal and, at least in the later members, were exclusively plant-eating.

Ornithischia (Table 2)
The ornithischians are the second major division of the dinosaurs. They are not directly related to the saurischians and in fact achieved their dinosaur status of upright posture and large size quite separately, although they must have originated from similar semiaquatic thecodont ancestors. In marked contrast to the saurischians the pubis pointed backwards in the manner of the bird pelvis, hence the name of the group which means bird-hipped. In the most primitive

Table 2

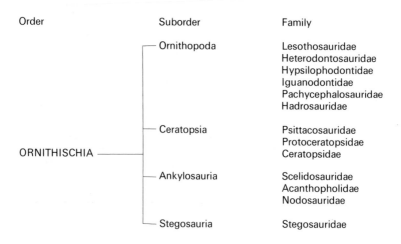

Order	Suborder	Family
	Ornithopoda	Lesothosauridae Heterodontosauridae Hypsilophodontidae Iguanodontidae Pachycephalosauridae Hadrosauridae
	Ceratopsia	Psittacosauridae Protoceratopsidae Ceratopsidae
ORNITHISCHIA	Ankylosauria	Scelidosauridae Acanthopholidae Nodosauridae
	Stegosauria	Stegosauridae

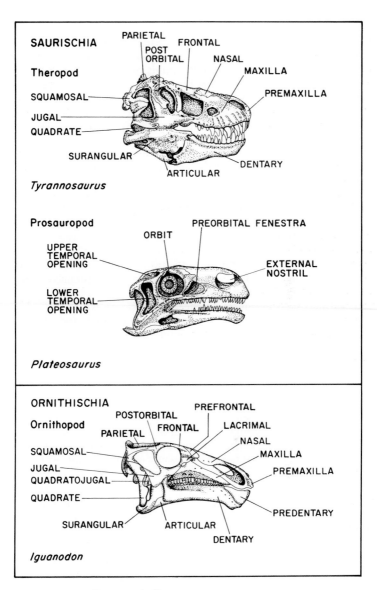

Representative dinosaur skulls.

members, the pubis seems simply to have been rotated so that it ran alongside the ischium but in the majority of forms there was the development of an anterior prepubic process, which is then associated with a later reduction of the pubis proper. This trend reaches its climax in the ceratopsians or horned dinosaurs where the pelvic girdle appears to be the same as a saurischian with the typical triradiate pelvis. Only a study of its precursors establishes that what appears to be an anteriorly directed pubis is in fact the strongly developed prepubis. It is recognised that a backwards pointing pubis is not a feature confined to the ornithischians; it took place in the birds and has also been recorded among some of the most advanced carnivorous saurischians.

There is one feature of the ornithischians which is, however, unique to them and that is the presence of a single median bone at the tip of the lower jaw – the predentary. The food gathering part of the jaw apparatus was a kind of beak and behind this was a grinding dentition. Apart from the most primitive examples, the side of the cheek region of the skull and the adjacent part of the lower jaw were concave and this is strong evidence of the former existence of cheek pouches, which means that the ornithischians were unique among reptiles in possessing muscular cheeks – a feature which they share with the mammals. Coupled with a grinding dentition and muscular cheeks, there was a tendency for the internal nostrils to be displaced more posteriorly and in some forms, notably the ankylosaurs, a solid secondary bony palate was formed which separated the food and air passages, in the same way that it does among the mammals. All these features demonstrate that the ornithischians were able to prepare their food for digestion in the mouth and breathe at the same time.

The ornithischians were exclusively herbivorous and they fall into four clearly defined groups. The main or central stock comprised the bipedal ornithopods, which during the Cretaceous gave rise to the secondarily quadrupedal horned dinosaurs or ceratopsians. In parallel with the ornithopods were the armoured dinosaurs or ankylosaurs which were primitively quadrupedal with a massive protective armour. These gave rise to the roofed dinosaurs or stegosaurs.

4
Theropoda – Beast-Footed Dinosaurs

All the bipedal carnivorous dinosaurs are included in the Theropoda. The neck is generally shorter than the trunk and the tibia or shin bone is longer than the femur. The hands bear sharp claws and there are two or three fingers only, the fourth and fifth fingers being either reduced or lost. In the feet there are three clawed toes; the fifth is always reduced while the first or big toe is shortened and turned backwards. There is a set of abdominal ribs which seem to have developed from the primitive bony armour of their ancestors. The theropods fall into two major divisions – a lightly built group, the Coelurosauria, and a more heavily built group, the Carnosauria.

Carnosauria

The heavily built flesh-eaters include the most primitive of all the dinosaurs, together with the largest land carnivore of all time *Tyrannosaurus*. In all cases the first toe points backwards and the main part of the foot is made up of three toes with the fifth being reduced or lost. There are four main families of carnosaur – the primitive armoured ornithosuchids, which gave rise first to the megalosaurs and then the sail-backed spinosaurs, and finally the giant tyrannosaurs.

ORNITHOSUCHIDAE

The ornithosuchids were the basic stock of the carnivorous dinosaurs and clearly show the fundamental structures of the first dinosaurs. In fact all the dinosaurs can be derived ultimately from just such ornithosuchid conditions.

Ornithosuchus longidens (1)

Ornithosuchus reached a length of 3.5m (11ft 6in) and specimens are known as small as 1m (3ft 3in) long. The skull was very pointed appearing almost beak-like with a battery of long backward curved teeth with serrated edges. The neck was short and the long muscular tail flattened from side to side. The forelimbs were about $\frac{2}{3}$ the length of the hind limbs. The hand was specialised for grasping and this dinosaur habitually walked on its hind limbs. In view of its bulk it is unlikely to have been able to run.

In between the nostril and orbit was a large opening called the preorbital fenestra, the margins of which formed a basin-like rim. This structure probably housed a salt gland. This is a specialisation characteristic of animals living in arid regions and enables the individuals to get rid of excess salt. Some living ocean-going birds such as fulmars can drink sea water and the excess salt is excreted through the salt gland which opens between the nostrils and eyes.

One of the striking features of *Ornithosuchus* was its armour of bony scutes beneath the skin. Over the trunk region, these were in the form of paired parallel rows running down the back. In the region of the tail the paired scutes were fused together to form a sharp serrated ridge along the top. The tail was flattened from side to side. In the neck region the paired rows of scutes developed sharp spines which projected upwards and both sideways and backwards. These spiny scutes would have provided protection for the vulnerable neck region especially from the younger and smaller individuals of some of the contemporary lightly-built carnivores.

Ornithosuchus inhabited a fairly arid region and preyed upon large, unarmoured, heavily built, sprawling, mollusc-eating rhynchosaur lizards such as *Hyperodapedon* and the armoured plant-eating advanced thecodont *Stagonolepis*. The young ornithosuchians probably fed on the small rhychocephalian lizard *Brachyrhinodon* and the lizard-like *Leptopleuron* as well as the small crocodile *Erpetosuchus*.

The modern reconstruction of the skeleton and skull of *Ornithosuchus* is based on a monographic study published in 1964 by A. D. Walker and this is a monument to his remarkable skill in studying probably the most difficult dinosaur fossils ever discovered. Most of the remains are preserved as holes in the rock. The bones have long since dissolved away simply leaving holes as the only evidence of their former existence. From the quarries all the rocks that had holes in them were collected and the holes filled with a flexible plastic material, which was then extracted to reveal the original shape of the bones. In this way after many years it was possible to put together a complete reconstruction of the skeleton.

Ornithosuchus is classified in its own family and included in the carnosaurs but it can be considered as the common ancestor to all the later carnosaurs, the megalosaurs and tyrannosaurs.

Ornithosuchus is known from the Elgin Sandstones Upper Triassic, of the Lossiemouth and Elgin region of N.E. Scotland.

The megalosaurs were the major family of the carnosaurs and were essentially larger versions of the ornithosuchids in which the bony armour had been lost. The hand bore three strongly clawed fingers while the 4th and 5th fingers were greatly reduced. The megalosaurs were the least specialised of all the large carnivorous dinosaurs. They possessed powerful sharp blade-like teeth with serrated edges, strong forearms and powerful hind-limbs, again bearing three large claws. The large muscular tail was flattened from side to side and served as a counterbalance for the head and trunk and kept the centre of gravity over the limb girdle and limbs.

The neck was short and powerful but nevertheless flexible. The megalosaurs were not capable of running but walked with fairly short strides after their prey. There are footprints known which seem to record a megalosaur stalking a large herbivorous dinosaur, at a speed of 8kph (5mph). The normal speed for the large megalosaurs was generally only about 4kph ($2\frac{1}{2}$mph). Megalosaurs occur in the lower Jurassic and continue until the end of the Cretaceous period in most parts of the world.

Yangchuanosaurus shangyauensis (III, 2)

Yangchuanosaurus was one of the smaller members of the megalosaur family. It had a flexible neck, as is evident from the way the head is twisted over the back in the photograph taken during the excavation of the skeleton. The position in death suggests that during life, as well as the neck being flexible, this dinosaur was capable of raising its tail. The position of the legs also demonstrates that it could take comparatively large strides and hence was likely to have been an active hunter. This dinosaur was described in 1978 and is one of the few complete skeletons known. It reveals important information regarding the range of different postures that must have been possible during life. This form lived in well vegetated lowland regions and preyed upon herbivores inhabiting low swampy ground. Living in such lush regions it was probably camouflaged and its colouring would have enabled it to blend into its surroundings. The lighter underside, in conjunction with the shadow from the upper surface, would have produced an overall impression of the same tone – an effect known as countershading. The dark patches on the dorsal surface would have served to break up the smooth outline of the animal and thus make it less conspicuous to its intended victims.

Yangchuanosaurus comes from Upper Jurassic rocks in Yangchuan District, Szechuan Province, E. China.

Megalosaurus bucklandi (3)

Megalosaurus was the major carnivore during the Jurassic and early Cretaceous in Europe. In most respects it was similar in proportions to *Ornithosuchus* and *Yangchuanosaurus*. There is some evidence that a few bony scutes were still present in the skin. The forelimbs with their three clawed fingers remained powerful and were used for tearing their prey. The teeth were continually replaced throughout life. The jaws, although narrow, did not come to a sharp beak-like point but were more rounded. The jaws and teeth were not used primarily for despatching the prey; the steak-knife saw-edged teeth were ideal for slicing off flesh once the victim was inert. The main weapons were the clawed hands and the even more powerful clawed feet. From the evidence of footprints it seems that the megalosaurs hunted in small groups. An average *Megalosaurus* was about 9m (30ft) in length, and as they were not able to move speedily it is likely that they were to a large extent scavengers.

Megalosaurus was first discovered in the Stonesfield Slate of the Upper Jurassic of Stonesfield near Oxford and further remains are known from Upper Jurassic and Wealden, Lower Cretaceous, rocks in England in Dorset, Gloucestershire, Wiltshire, Yorkshire, Kent, Sussex and the Isle of Wight. Remains attributed to *Megalosaurus* have been reported from Australia, East Africa (Tanzania), France, Portugal and India but further research is required for these identifications to be confirmed.

Allosaurus fragilis (4)

The original name of this dinosaur, *Antrodemus*, was based on half a tail vertebra. Later parts of a skeleton in which the tail was missing were discovered and named *Allosaurus fragilis*. At the time there was no way of deciding if these two sets of remains belonged to the same or different dinosaurs. Subsequently complete skeletons were excavated which suggested that the half a tail bone belonged to the same type of dinosaur that had become known as *Allosaurus*. This meant that as only one name should be used *Antrodemus* was the correct name for this giant 11m (36ft) long, 2 tonne, flesh-eater. The most recent study, in 1976, has concluded that the original tail vertebra is unidentifiable, and so now the valid name is again *Allosaurus*.

One of the main differences from *Megalosaurus* is that *Allosaurus* has five pairs of teeth in the premaxilla bone of the upper jaw, whereas *Megalosaurus* has four pairs. One other feature that distinguishes *Allosaurus* is that there is a second opening in the side of the skull between the nostrils and the preorbital fenestra (which housed the salt gland). There are other parts of the skull which characterise *Allosaurus*: running from between the eyes to the tip of the snout there is a narrow vertical ridge and in front of the eyes standing up above the salt gland structure there is a pair of triangular projections. Behind the eyes there is a further pair but not quite as prominent. These skull decorations give *Allosaurus* a characteristic shape to its head.

Allosaurus fed on such herbivorous dinosaurs as the giant semi-aquatic sauropods like *Apatosaurus* (*Brontosaurus*). It is not known whether they were active hunters. They were more probably scavengers. In any case there is direct evidence from the preserved remains of the tail of an *Apatosaurus*. The processes of the tail bones are broken off and the bones themselves have been scored as if by knives. The spacing of these breaks and the scoring is exactly the spacing of the teeth of *Allosaurus*. Moreover a number of broken *Allosaurus* teeth were found alongside this same tail. The fact that *Allosaurus* had bothered to feed on a brontosaur tail is strong evidence that it must have been scavenging. If it had killed this dinosaur there would have been a vast amount of more easily accessible meat available.

From the evidence of footprints it was discovered for the first time in 1980 that such dinosaurs as *Allosaurus* were capable of swimming and hence they were able to reach the swamp dwelling sauropods.

Allosaurus occurs in the Como Bluff Quarries of the Morrison Formation, Upper Jurassic, of Wyoming and in Colorado.

Ceratosaurus nasicornis (5)

A contemporary of *Allosaurus* inhabiting the same environment was the megalosaur *Ceratosaurus*. This dinosaur was only 6m (20ft) in length and was a swifter hunter and, from the evidence of footprints, appears to have hunted in packs. The occurrence of numerous parallel trackways can only be explained if a group had crossed the patch of ground at the same time together – individuals by themselves could never produce such perfect parallel trackways. It is likely that the packs of relatively small, by dinosaur standards, *Ceratosaurus* represented the active hunters and after a kill the lumbering *Allosaurus* would come on the scene, drive off the *Ceratosaurus* pack and consume what was left.

The most striking feature of *Ceratosaurus* was the pointed horn above its nose. There were also a pair of projections above and in front of the eyes. The nasal horn was not a weapon, the clawed hands and feet performed this function. The horn was a display structure, which could have been used in trials of strength between members of the same species. By such means a peck-order would be established in the pack without any serious injury ever being inflicted. *Ceratosaurus* was one of the few megalosaurs possessing a row of bony scutes running along the midline of the back.

Ceratosaurus is found in the Morrison Formation, Upper Jurassic, of Colorado and Wyoming.

Dilophosaurus weatherilli (6)

Dilophosaurus was one of the earliest members of the megalosaurs and is known from a perfectly preserved skeleton. The most remarkable feature of this flesh-eater is the pair of paper thin bony plates which form a crest running from the back of the head as far as the nostrils. At the posterior margin, these crests form a pair of sharp spines pointing backwards. The thin bony sheets have vertical struts of bone strengthening them. The possession of such delicate bony structures on the top of the head seems to be difficult to explain. It indicates that when *Dilophosaurus* was actively engaged in dealing with its prey, it would not have brought its jaw apparatus into play as the delicate crests would have been easily damaged. This implies that *Dilophosaurus* used only its limbs in the task of killing its victims. There is, however, a possibility that the crests may not have belonged to the complete skeleton that was found. In the rocks where this material was excavated the delicate bony crests were not actually found attached to the skull of the skeleton and so they may have belonged to some other dinosaur as yet undiscovered. The association of these structures in the vicinity of the megalosaur skeleton is suggestive of their association in life; and, although photographs of the skeleton with the crest attached have been published and make it appear convincing, it is important to remember that they were not actually found together.

Dilophosaurus comes from the Kayenta Sandstone, Lower Jurassic, of Arizona.

SPINOSAURIDAE

The spinosaur dinosaurs were an unusual development of the carnosaurs and were characterised by the enormous increase in the length of the dorsal spines of the vertebrae of the main part of the back. This remarkable structure formed a huge rigid sail structure which must have been especially vulnerable for an active carnivore. Primitive members of this family have been discovered in the Upper Jurassic, and during the succeeding Cretaceous period the sails became progressively exaggerated culminating in the 12m (40ft) long *Spinosaurus*.

Spinosaurus aegypticus (7)

The evolution of the sail-back dinosaurs reached its peak in *Spinosaurus*. Some of the vertical spines of the vertebrae were 1.9m (6ft 3in) in height and in life these spines would have been covered by a sheet of skin well supplied with blood vessels. The mere presence of such a large rigid sail on the back of this dinosaur meant that it was unlikely ever to have come into violent conflict with either its own kind or its prey. In view also of its massive size, it could not have been particularly active and so, like the larger megalosaurs, it is most likely to have been a scavenger. It appears that it inhabited open country and one of the serious problems that such an animal would have had to face in these conditions would have been long exposure to direct sunlight. In view of the comparatively small area of skin relative to the volume of the body, there would have been no way of getting rid of excess heat. The role of the sail was to provide a large surface area well supplied with blood vessels in the skin, which would have served as an effective cooling device. By the same token, should it ever have been required, it could have also served as a kind of solar heating panel. By orientating the sail towards the sun in the early morning it could have gained the full impact of the sun's rays, while during the heat of the day, if the dinosaur faced the sun, the sail would have been end on and would in this position have functioned as a cooling device. This specialisation survived into the middle of the Cretaceous period and then this group became extinct.

Spinosaurus comes from the Baharia Formation of the Cretaceous (Cenomanian) of Egypt.

Altispinax dunkeri

Remains of a smaller spined dinosaur are known from the Lower Cretaceous Wealden rocks of Sussex as well as from Belgium and Hannover, Germany. In *Altispinax* the vertebral spines were about four times as long as the individual vertebrae. This dinosaur is thought to have been the possible ancestor of the giant *Spinosaurus*.

Metriacanthosaurus parkeri

A number of fragmentary skeletal remains have been discovered from the Oxford Clay, Jurassic, of Weymouth, Dorset, and these show the spines of the vertebrae extending to about twice the length of the vertebrae. This dinosaur seems to have been the ancestral spinosaur and shows the very beginning of the sail-back trend.

The tyrannosaurs mark the very peak of the evolution of the carnosaurs, culminating in the largest terrestrial flesh-eater of all time, *Tyrannosaurus rex*. The skulls were massively constructed and the jaws were comparatively short and deep. The neck and trunk region was shorter in proportion than in the megalosaurs and the heavy muscular tail was held more or less horizontally. One of the most surprising aspects of the tyrannosaurs was the reduction in the size of the forelimbs and the loss of all but two fingers. Although the young tyrannosaurs could have been active hunters, the adults were slow moving ponderous scavengers.

Tyrannosaurus rex (8)

Tyrannosaurus rex is one of the most popular of all the dinosaurs by virtue of its size, being some 12m (40ft) long and weighing about 6 tonnes in life, and also by its evocative name meaning 'king of the tyrant reptiles'. In spite of its familiarity not a single complete skeleton has ever been found. The famous mounted skeleton in the American Museum of Natural History in New York is composed of several partial skeletons and it is on this reconstruction that the majority of restorations of *Tyrannosaurus* have been based. The backbone in this reconstruction sloped at an angle of about 45 degrees and the long tail curled round near its tip. The actual curving of the tail was because there was not enough room in the exhibition hall for it to be put on display with the tail kept straight, as it should have been. The acquisition of a cast of a skull and a partial skeleton by the British Museum (Natural History) in London led to a new study of *Tyrannosaurus* by B. H. Newman and he showed that the famous restoration had been given a tail that was over 3m (10ft) too long. From a study of the vertebrae of the back it was evident that the main part of the body, and also the tail, must have been habitually held in the horizontal plane. The neck vertebrae were quite different and proved that *Tyrannosaurus* had a very flexible neck that rose almost at right angles to the back. On the basis of this new study the reconstruction that Newman produced showed *Tyrannosaurus* standing in a completely different manner to that seen in all the older versions.

The next stage was the realisation from an examination of the limbs and pelvic girdle that *Tyrannosaurus* was incapable of taking large strides. In fact its stride was not much longer than the length of its foot. This proves that *Tyrannosaurus* was a very slow moving dinosaur and not able to walk at much more than 5kph (3mph), less than the speed of a man walking. This re-study of *Tyrannosaurus* demonstrated that in spite of its terrifying appearance this dinosaur could not have been an active hunter, it could only have been a scavenger. The long 150mm (6in) blade-like teeth which were ideal for cutting up meat show signs of wear, but this could only be because they were used on inert material. The teeth could not have been brought into action when the prey was alive as their fragility would have resulted in their snapping off. This dental evidence is again consistent with a scavenging mode of life.

The enormous reduction of the forelimbs to produce arms that appear ridiculously small and completely out of proportion to the rest of the body, and the reduction of the hand to two small fingers, have until recently presented a problem, as they would have been useless for dealing with prey. Newman has shown that in fact they played a very important role in the life of *Tyrannosaurus*. When the animal was lying down on the ground with its hind limbs folded, any attempt to straighten the legs in order to lift the body would have simply pushed the head and trunk along the ground. The function of the clawed hand was to stick in the ground to prevent this forwards sliding so that the force extending the hind limbs could be transmitted to lifting the dinosaur.

Tyrannosaurus material is best known from the Hell Creek Formation of the Upper Cretaceous of Montana.

Albertosaurus sternbergi
Among the last of the carnivorous dinosaurs were a number of tyrannosaurs and isolated skeletal remains of these have been found since the 1850s, all of which were given different names by the first scientists to describe them. One of the best preserved skeletons was named *Gorgosaurus sternbergi*, a fine mounted skeleton of which is on display in the Field Museum in Chicago. Since this discovery it has been claimed that *Gorgosaurus* is the same as *Deinodon* and also *Aublysodon* and these names have replaced *Gorgosaurus* in some books. The view now generally held by most dinosaur experts is that the name should in fact be *Albertosaurus*. This tyrannosaur was only about 8m (26ft) in length and comes from the Old Man Formation, Upper Cretaceous, from the Deer River area of Alberta, Canada.

Tarbosaurus efremovi (II, VI)
During a number of Soviet Expeditions to the Gobi desert in Mongolia after World War 2 a number of well preserved tyrannosaur skeletons were excavated and several of these are on display in the Palaeontological Institute Museum of the Academy of Science in

Two skeletons of Tarbosaurus *as preserved in the rock (from R. Gradzinski)*

Moscow. They are displayed with the same pattern of sloping back and long striding gait as the original American reconstruction. Similarly the tails have been unduly lengthened in the same way as in the American version. Nevertheless, these remains are especially important as they establish that the tyrannosaurs were established in Mongolia as well as in North America. The Mongolian tyrannosaurs appear to be of a somewhat lighter build than *Tyrannosaurus* itself but some Russian workers now consider that *Tarbosaurus* should be included in the genus *Tyrannosaurus*.

A fairly complete skeleton of *Tarbosaurus* was excavated by the 1967–1971 Polish-Mongolian Expeditions which showed the vertebrae of the tail and back forming a rigid horizontal line, and the head raised on a highly flexible neck. A further partially articulated skeleton showed that the anterior part of the tail was straight and in line with the back but that the tail became much more flexible towards its tip. The importance of these specimens is that they provided the first conclusive evidence of the length of a tyrannosaur tail and dramatically confirmed the correctness of Newman's new restoration.

Tarbosaurus comes from the Nemegt Beds, Upper Cretaceous, of the Nemegt Basin, Mongolia.

Coelurosauria

The second major division of the carnivorous theropod dinosaurs consists of the lightly built coelurosaurs. They have delicate thin-walled bones and long necks and tails. The orbits are particularly large and the skulls are generally long and slender. The shin bone, or tibia, is always much longer than the femur and the foot bones, or metatarsals, are also much elongated. Although the forelimbs are shorter than the hind limbs they are nevertheless long and slender with particularly long clawed fingers. There are two families of coelurosaur – the primitive procompsognathids and the more ad-vanced coelurids. From the coelurosaur stock there evolved two further groups of highly specialised lightly built carnivorous dino-saurs which used to be classified within the coelurosaurs. However, they seem to have developed sufficiently far from the basic coelur-osaur pattern that they are now placed in two separate groups of equal rank to the coelurosaurs. These are the sickle-clawed dinosaurs or deinonychosaurs and the ostrich dinosaurs or ornithomimosaurs. Finally there is now evidence that the coelurosaurs gave rise to a further group that is sufficiently different in certain features that not only is it not classified as a coelurosaur but not even as a reptile and instead is placed in a separate class, Aves – the birds.

PROCOMPSOGNATHIDAE
The most primitive members of the coelurosaurs which occur in rocks of Upper Triassic age are usually grouped together in this family. The best known specimens come from Germany, Scotland and eastern North America. Most of the early forms were less than a metre in length and in many regions of the world have left evidence of their former presence in the form of footprints. Among the most famous were the bird-like trackways preserved in the Triassic sandstones of the Connecticut Valley which at the beginning of the last century were popularly supposed to have been made by 'Noah's Ravens'. In the 1970s similar coelurosaur tracks were discovered near Cardiff in South Wales and these showed that these dinosaurs were walking across the area at about 8kph (5mph).

Procompsognathus triassicus (9)
Procompsognathus is one of the most primitive of all the coelurosaurs; the hands still retain five fingers although the 4th and 5th fingers are somewhat reduced. The tibia is only a little longer than the femur. The hind foot has three main toes (the 2nd, 3rd and 4th), the first toe points backwards and the fifth is missing. A further aspect of the primitive nature of this dinosaur is the fact that there are only three sacral vertebrae. This means that the pelvic girdle was only attached

to the backbone via three specialised vertebrae. There are a number of other similar dinosaurs that have been at one time or another classified with *Procompsognathus* but some such as *Hallopus* have since been discovered to be lightly built running crocodiles.

Procompsognathus comes from the Stubensandstein, Keuper Sandstones, Upper Triassic, of North Wurttenberg, Germany.

Saltopus elginensis (10)

Saltopus was one of the smallest dinosaurs with a length of under a metre. It was a very slender individual and is known from a partial skeleton which unfortunately is missing the skull. There are still five fingers on the hand but the 4th and 5th are greatly reduced. The strengthening of the pelvic girdle is more advanced in that there are now four sacral vertebrae. This tiny dinosaur lived in the same conditions as the primitive carnosaur *Ornithosuchus* and would probably have preyed on its hatchlings. Like the other coelurosaurs its success was due to its being fleet of foot.

Saltopus occurs in the Stagonolepis Sandstone of the Upper Triassic, from Elgin, N.E. Scotland.

Coelophysis bauri (11)

Coelophysis is one of the larger members of the primitive coelurosaurs reaching a maximum length of nearly 3m (10ft) although individuals only 1m (3ft 3in) long are known. This dinosaur shows still further improvements on the other members of the family. The sacrum is now made up of five vertebrae, a character which marks the more advanced coelurosaurs of the succeeding Jurassic period.

Perhaps the most important aspect of *Coelophysis* is that it is by far the most completely known of all the coelurosaurs. Dozens of complete skeletons are known including all growth stages from individuals 1m in length up to the largest just under 3m. The skull is very long and delicate with numerous small teeth. The neck is very long and flexible enough for the head to reach the pelvic region. The tail is enormously long and, although the individual vertebrae are themselves long, the end is again flexible. The arms are about half the length of the hind limbs and there are three long clawed fingers. The fifth finger is missing and the fourth reduced to a vestige without any sign of a claw.

Coelophysis used to be classified in the family based on *Podekosaurus holyokensis* from the Portland Formation of the Newark Sandstones, Upper Triassic, of Massachusetts, but in 1947 E. H. Colbert excavated the site where the original fragments of *Coelophysis* had been discovered in 1881. Colbert's excavation uncovered dozens upon dozens of *Coelophysis* skeletons all piled on top of one another, all complete and intertwined. In the American Museum of Natural History, New York, there is on display a slab with two perfect specimens shown in their position of death and in numerous museums around the world a cast of one of these is generally to be seen. This gives the impression of one or two individuals having died and then been buried with little subsequent disturbance. In fact the original slab contains numerous individuals most of which have been carefully covered up so that only two specimens are to be seen. Had the original collection all been left exposed, it would have been difficult to make out any single skeleton amid the utter confusion of bones. The significance of this find is that it suggested that these lightly built flesh-eaters lived together in large groups. This was the conclusion that could have been drawn from the numerous trackways of their footprints but this was confirmed by Colbert's discovery. In some cases, however, there was evidence of cannibalism among these dinosaurs. It appears that a number had recently fed upon young individuals of their own kind.

Coelophysis occurs in the Petrified Forest Member of the Chinle Formation of the Upper Triassic, from Arroyo Seco, Ghost Ranch, north west of Abiquiu, New Mexico.

Syntarsus rhodesiensis

Part of a skeleton of a small dinosaur very similar to *Coelophysis* has been described from Upper Triassic sandstones near the Kwengula River some 30km north west of Bulawayo in Zimbabwe. The main difference seems to be in the fusion of some of the bones of the ankle joint and it may well be that this is simply due to this individual dinosaur suffering from a slight case of arthritis. *Syntarsus* remains are incomplete but in spite of this it has been used as the basis for a curious imaginative restoration. The head is portrayed as extremely long and there are feathery structures projecting in a plume from the back of the head. The tail is long and thin and rather rat-like and the entire body is covered in feathery scales. There is in fact no evidence whatsoever to support any of these aspects of this restoration even though it is frequently reproduced.

COELURIDAE

The later advanced coelurosaurs from the Jurassic period are grouped together in the coelurids, which are characterised by having no more than three clawed fingers on each hand. The dinosaur on which this family is based has the first digit facing the other two. Previously this family included all the more advanced coelurosaurs from the

Cretaceous with the exception of the ostrich dinosaurs. The discovery of the sickle clawed *Deinonychus* has lead to a re-examination of the later coelurosaurs and many of them are now excluded from the coelurids and placed in a new major grouping. Whether the coelurids in fact continued throughout the Cretaceous or gave rise to the deinonychosaurs without any of the original family continuing unchanged (which seems highly unlikely) will have to await future researches.

Coelurus hermani (12)

At the beginning of the present century H. F. Osborn described a small coelurosaur skeleton which he named *Ornitholestes hermani*. Its length was a little over 2m (6$\frac{1}{2}$ft) and its thumb with its claw faced the other two fingers. This lightly built dinosaur was hence clearly adapted for grasping objects and the name *Ornitholestes* which means 'bird robber' emphasised this presumed facility. The hint in the name suggested that this dinosaur caught birds and since that time artist after artist has portrayed this particular dinosaur grasping the first bird *Archaeopteryx* in its hands.

Such a situation might well have taken place but this dinosaur is known from North America and to date *Archaeopteryx* has only been found in Europe. Unfortunately it was later discovered that remains discovered and named *Coelurus* in the 1880s belonged to the same kind of dinosaur as *Ornitholestes* and so the evocative name has had to be replaced by *Coelurus*. *Coelurus* may well have been the ancestor of some of the later coelurosaur derivatives such as the ostrich dinosaurs. A striking feature is that the coelurid hands as well as the feet were remarkably similar to those of the first bird *Archaeopteryx*.

Coelurus comes from the aptly named Bone Cabin Quarry in the Morrison Formation, Upper Jurassic, of Wyoming.

Compsognathus longipes (13)

Until the discovery in 1972 of a further specimen from the south of France this dinosaur was only known from a single individual, perfectly preserved in the Lithographic Limestone of southern Germany. The original skeleton was first described in 1861 and recently J. H. Ostrom completed a re-examination of this specimen spending a whole year to accomplish the task, his results being published in 1978. *Compsognathus* was about 60mm (2ft) long, would have weighed between 3 and 3.5kg (6$\frac{1}{2}$–7$\frac{3}{4}$lb) and must have been about the size of a hen. The skeleton is preserved with the neck twisted back so that the skull is lying upside down with the tip of the snout resting by the base of the tail, which itself has been lifted upwards. For a long time this particular specimen was thought to represent the convulsions of the dinosaur's last minutes as it died from tetanus or some similar ailment, which produces such contortions of the back. This identical posture, however, is found in *Yangchuanosaurus*, *Dilophosaurus*, *Tarbosaurus* and *Coelophysis* and it is stretching credulity too far to postulate that all these died in such a manner. In fact this particular posture is likely to have occurred after death. Once the flesh had rotted away the surviving ligaments and tendons would have contracted and in so doing would have pulled the head and neck backwards and the tail upwards. Such movements, if not quite so extreme, would have been possible to a certain degree during life. It is evident that the main part of the trunk and the base of the tail formed a rigid horizontal unit but that the neck was flexible and so was the main part of the tail, albeit to a lesser extent.

The skeleton of *Compsognathus* also provided important evidence on the feeding habits of this dinosaur. It has been known for a long time that there were some minute bones preserved within the ribcage and these have been the subject of much speculation. It is only now with Ostrom's definitive study that they have at last been positively identified as belonging to *Bavarisaurus macrodactylus*, which was a lizard with an exceptionally long tail related to the common ancestry of the iguanas and gekkos. The fact that this dinosaur was able to hunt lizards successfully proves that it was an exceptionally fast and accurate hunter.

Compsognathus' major claim to fame has been its close similarity to the first bird *Archaeopteryx* which occurs in the same Lithographic Limestone. Both animals were identical in size and their gaits must have been indistinguishable. In the majority of parts of the skeleton they are virtually identical. The pubic bone of the pelvic girdle points forwards in *Compsognathus* as in normal coelurosaurs but backwards in *Archaeopteryx*; and there is a second preorbital fenestra in *Compsognathus* whereas there is only one in *Archaeopteryx*. One of the results of Ostrom's new study has been the realisation that *Compsognathus* differed from all other known coelurosaurs by only having two clawed fingers. This highly specialised hand makes it impossible for *Archaeopteryx* to be derived from *Compsognathus* itself, although it does not exclude the possibility of it having evolved from a close ancestor of *Compsognathus* that had not yet developed this two fingered specialisation.

Compsognathus comes from the Solenhofen Lithographic Limestone of the Upper Jurassic, near Kelheim, Bavaria, Germany.

BIRDS

Archaeopteryx lithographica (14)

The first bird *Archaeopteryx* is included at this point on the grounds that it is here that it fits into the general picture of the dinosaurs. All available evidence suggests that it was a specialised side-branch of the coelurids and was anatomically close to both *Coelurus* itself as well as to *Compsognathus*. Had the original specimens not been preserved with the detailed impressions of typical bird feathers, there would never have been any hesitation in including the skeleton of *Archaeopteryx* within the coelurid family of the coelurosaurs. The possession of feathers makes *Archaeopteryx* a true bird but there are further features which are also bird-like. There is a wishbone, formed by the fusion of the two clavicles or collar bones, the braincase is expanded in a bird-like manner and it now appears that the hollow bones contained air spaces, that the bone was pneumatic. The foot of *Archaeopteryx* was bird-like but so too were the feet of all the coelurosaurs. The rows of socketed teeth, the long bony tail and the three long fingers bearing claws are all typical coelurosaur features and are not at all bird-like.

When the features of *Archaeopteryx* are considered together there can be little doubt that such an animal represents the beginning of the birds; even the number of primary and secondary feathers on the wings are identical to those of all living birds. But it is equally evident that *Archaeopteryx* retained a large number of features from its reptilian ancestors such as the socketed teeth and long bony tail. From a detailed examination of all the features of the skeleton it seems that the most likely origin of *Archaeopteryx* and hence the birds was among the coelurid dinosaurs.

The five known specimens of *Archaeopteryx* come from the Solenhofen Lithographic Limestone, Upper Jurassic, of southern Germany.

Deinonychosauria

DROMAEOSAURIDAE

The deinonychosaurs were an important, if not the most important, element of the carnivorous dinosaurs of the Cretaceous period, a time which experienced the greatest variation of the dinosaurs. The deinonychosaurs were all lightly built and previously were included within the coleurosaurs, in particular in the coelurids, but recent discoveries have revealed that they had developed a number of remarkable specialisations which make it inappropriate to retain them within this classification, and instead they are grouped in a major division of their own of equal rank to the coelurosaurs, out of which they evolved. The dinosaurs of this newly recognised group are known as the clawed dinosaurs on account of the enormous development of the claw of the second toe which acted as a weapon for tearing open their prey. The forelimbs were longer than those of normal coelurosaurs, always being more than half the length of the hind limb. The ankle joint was shorter than in coleurosaurs, which suggests that they may not have been such good runners. The long clawed hands were specialised for grasping and holding. When taken in conjunction with the huge sickle-shaped second toe which was an organ devoted solely to slashing and tearing, a picture emerges of an active killer dinosaur, entirely distinct from the ponderous giant scavengers. The deinonychosaurs grabbed their victims with their hands and then, standing on one foot, disembowelled them. When running or walking these clawed dinosaurs only used two toes (the third and fourth), the sickle claw was kept raised off the ground and only brought into use in attack. In view of their active predatory ways these dinosaurs must have been exceptionally well adapted for balancing, considering they would often have had to deal with struggling prey while standing on one leg. The tails appear to have developed into sophisticated balancing organs. From about the tenth vertebra of the tail the individual bones were bound together by long thin rods of bone so that the tail acted as a balancing pole, being straight and rigid. However, the vertebrae were capable of a slight degree of movement so that the tail would have had the same kind of flexibility as a bamboo stick. The long rods of bone running along the tail appear at first glance to be ossified tendons and ligaments but when examined more closely they are seen to be elongated extensions of the articulating processes of the vertebrae themselves, the post and pre-zygapophyses. On the undersurface of the vertebrae are small Y shaped bones, the chevrons, and these similarly are drawn out into long rods.

The specialisations of the skeleton are so advanced compared with the ancestral group that it seems entirely justified to place them in an independent group of the carnivorous dinosaurs. All the features of these clawed dinosaurs point to a highly active way of life. They were the 'big cats' of the world of the dinosaurs lying in wait and then leaping onto their victims, which they tore apart with their specialised ripping claws.

A re-examination of the lightly built carnivorous dinosaurs of the Cretaceous period has so far shown that four main types can be identified as deinonychosaurs. They are so far only known with certainty from Mongolia and western North America. This was at the time when eastern Asia and western America were united to form a single continent, so it is not surprising that the same types of dinosaur are found today in both these areas.

Deinonychus antirrhopus (15)

Deinonychus was described in 1969 in a comprehensive monograph by J. H. Ostrom. In life it was between 3 and 4m (10–13ft) long and was the largest member of this group to which it has given its name. Originally this dinosaur was thought to be a unique specialisation among the dinosaurs but now it is known that there were other such clawed dinosaurs, which survived until the end of the Cretaceous period. By far the most striking feature of *Deinonychus* was its foot. Whereas in all other carnivorous dinosaurs the third toe was the longest with the second and fourth being considerably shorter, in the case of *Deinonychus* the fourth toe was almost the same length as the third and the dinosaur walked and ran on only these two toes. The first toe was short and, although it bore a small sharp claw, this pointed backwards as in the carnosaurs and coelurosaurs. The second toe bore a huge sickle-like claw from which the animal gets its name, 'terrible claw'. Unlike the toes of any other dinosaurs this one could be bent back so that when the animal stood or walked it would be raised clear of the ground. At the same time this claw could be swung through a very large arc and when brought into play, such as when disembowelling its prey, would be driven backwards with the full power of the entire limb. For this highly evolved weapon to have been used effectively *Deinonychus* must have been able to use one foot while standing on the other and this implies a remarkably well developed sense of balance. The hands, too, illustrate further developments for an active predatory mode of life. The long clawed fingers of the hand turned towards each other, which means that *Deinonychus* could have grasped its prey effectively. This ability was better developed than in any kind of dinosaur, as the hands were able to rotate on the wrist, a feature not known among other reptiles. A further specialisation again related to its mode of life is seen in the tail which was stiffened by numerous long bony rods. These rods were elongated parts of the vertebrae themselves and they projected forwards so that most of them extend the length of ten vertebrae. This means that in parts of the tail an individual vertebra would have been surrounded by 40 rods of bone. This arrangement would have produced one of the most rigid tails in the animal kingdom. Nevertheless, a slight degree of movement was possible. In most dinosaurs the main movement of the tail was from side to side but in

Deinonychus it was up and down. It functioned as a balancing, stabilising organ.

All these specialisations provided a completely new insight into the range of behaviour among the dinosaurs. Here was a dinosaur with an agility that was completely unexpected, which suggested that the tempo of life was vastly more energetic than was previously imagined. The existence of leaping and pouncing dinosaurs even led some scientists to believe that these dinosaurs were so advanced that they should no longer be classified as reptiles but should be placed in a separate class of vertebrates equal in rank to birds and mammals.

One further piece of evidence regarding the mode of life of *Deinonychus* was the discovery of the remains of about five individuals with a large herbivore weighing about six times as much as a single *Deinonychus*. It may well be that *Deinonychus* hunted in packs just as some of the large cats do today and were thus able to tackle prey very much larger than themselves.

Deinonychus comes from the Cloverly Formation from the Late Aptian or early Albian of the Lower Cretaceous of south central Montana.

Saurornithoides mongoliensis (16)

Saurornithoides was one of the last representatives of the deinonychosaurs and was notable in that the second toe, instead of being developed into a large sickle shaped weapon, was much reduced. Its arms, however, were probably more manoeuvrable than those of *Deinonychus*. The skull was much longer with small serrated teeth but the most obvious features were the enormous eyes. The size and position of the eyes were such that both were able to focus on the same object. The dinosaur had binocular vision and this in conjunction with its long grasping hands adapted it perfectly for locating small prey and snatching it up. It is considered that *Saurornithoides* preyed upon lizards and small mammals, and the size of its eyes suggests that it hunted mammals during the twilight hours as the light was fading. It does not seem to have been a leaping, slashing dinosaur but a stealthy crepuscular hunter of small mammals that came out to feed as the night approached. As well as the enormous development of the eyes *Saurornithoides* was notable for the large size of its brain. It was as large, relatively, as the brain of the present day large flightless birds such as the ostrich and this indicates that its pattern of behaviour and feeding was much more complex than that of its contemporary dinosaurian relatives. When the relative brain sizes of all the more advanced lightly built carnivorous dinosaurs are compared with other reptiles, that is the living forms as well as the other dinosaurs, they appear to be significantly different. If one takes the brain-to-body ratio for crocodiles throughout the known range of crocodile sizes as unit 1 then all the quadrupedal dinosaurs have a lower ratio of relative size of brain, with the brontosaurs coming at the bottom with about a quarter of that amount. The main bipedal dinosaurs, the flesh-eating carnosaurs and the bipedal herbivorous ornithischians range from 1 to 2. Using this same criterion the lightly built carnivorous dinosaurs have a score of 5.75 − nearly six times greater brain power than living crocodiles. In fact the deinonychians' brain-to-body ratios fall completely outside the range of all living reptiles and all other dinosaurs but within the range of birds. The large relative brain size together with the skeletal evidence of the hunting behaviour of these dinosaurs suggests that these particular dinosaurs had reached a higher level of organisation than that normally associated with reptiles.

Saurornithoides comes from the Djadokta Formation of the Upper Cretaceous of Bayn Dzak, Mongolia. A similar dinosaur from Canada based on less complete material was named *Stenonychosaurus inequalis* but this seems to be indistinguishable from *Saurornithoides* and hence the Canadian form should be included in the genus *Saurornithoides*.

Velociraptor mongoliensis (17)

Velociraptor is a small deinonychosaur which still retains the important sickle claw as its major weapon for dealing with its prey. This dinosaur has achieved fame because in 1971 a complete skeleton was discovered in Mongolia in association with the herbivorous *Protoceratops*. Both had perished at the very moment of *Velociraptor's* attack on *Protoceratops*. Perhaps the most amazing aspect of this find is that it confirmed in the most dramatic manner imaginable the method of attack that Ostrom had postulated from his analysis of the bones of *Deinonychus*. *Velociraptor* was grasping the head of *Protoceratops* in its hands; the sickle claw of the foot was in the very act of tearing into the body, although in this instance it seems to have caught the edge of the head armour, allowing the beak of *Protoceratops* to attack the chest of the predator. Whatever the actual details of this fatal encounter both dinosaurs succumbed, locked together in this embrace of death.

Velociraptor was discovered in the Djadochta Formation of the Upper Cretaceous, of Shabarak Usu, Mongolia.

Dromaeosaurus albertensis (18)

Dromaeosaurus was one of the first examples of this type of dinosaur to be discovered and has given its name to the family in which they are all included. This form was similar to *Velociraptor* although it lived at a later period and is known from Canada.

Dromaeosaurus remains have been found in the Oldman Formation, Upper Cretaceous, of Red Deer River, Alberta, Canada.

Deinocheirosauria
DEINOCHEIRIDAE
Deinocheirus mirificus (19)
Deinocheirus or 'terrible hand' is one of the most enigmatic of dinosaurs. It is known from the remains of two arms, which were 2.5m (8ft) long ending in hands bearing three gigantic claws. There is absolutely no information at all with regard to what the rest of the body was like. There is no way of telling whether this dinosaur with its vicious looking hands had disproportionate sized arms or whether its body was utterly gigantic. The size of these arms is so far outside the range of any known carnivorous dinosaur that these unique remains are placed in an independent group. Only future discoveries will solve the puzzle of these strange and terrifying hands.

Deinocheirus comes from the Upper Nemegt Formation of the Upper Cretaceous from Altan Ula, in the Nemegt Basin, Mongolia.

Ornithomimosauria
ORNITHOMIMIDAE
The carnivorous dinosaurs, again from a coelurid stock, gave rise during the Cretaceous period to a further highly specialised group – the ostrich dinosaurs. These dinosaurs are characterised by their long spindly legs which have three toes. The first toe which, in all the other carnivorous forms, projects backwards, is completely missing. The forelimbs are also long and slender with exceptionally long fingers well adapted for grasping objects, although the first fingers did not oppose the other two. The neck was long and thin and was surmounted by a small delicate skull. The bones of the skull were almost paper thin and, most unusual of all, there were no teeth. The lower jaw itself was very slender. The long tail was held horizontally in line with the rigid back, the neck was long and flexible with the delicate head held at right angles to it. The normal standing posture was comparable to that of the large flightless birds such as the ostrich. Even the height of these dinosaurs was similar, their length being 3 to 4m (10–13ft) although some were as small as 2m (6½ft). With these features it is difficult to imagine that they could have been active aggressive carnivores in the same sense as the deinonychosaurs.

From the proportions of the hind limbs they were clearly fast runners and would always have been capable of escaping the attentions of any enemies. The mode of life to which these dinosaurs were successfully adapted is something of a mystery. By far the most popular and perhaps most likely theory is that they preyed upon the eggs of other dinosaurs. Their height and good eyesight would have enabled them to spy out likely nesting sites and their hands would have been able to hold an egg. With their long legs they would have made good their escape from enraged parents and with the sharp bird-like beak they would have been well able to break into the dinosaur eggs.

The ostrich dinosaurs are known from the Upper Cretaceous of North America and Asia.

Ornithomimus velox (20)

Ornithomimus was first recognised from rather fragmentary remains in 1890 but even then it was clear that they belonged to a dinosaur which in many respects, especially the delicate toothless jaws, mimicked large flightless birds. Subsequently complete skeletons were discovered so that the general, rather ostrich-like, appearance was confirmed. The basic plan of the skeleton was very similar in all the ornithomimosaurs – the long tail was usually held horizontally as was the trunk, the neck with its relatively tiny head was raised up in the manner more or less of ostriches. The forelimbs were unusual in their length, although still shorter than the long spindly hind limbs. *Ornithomimus* seems to have inhabited dense cypress swamps and forests and is hence likely to have been darkly coloured, otherwise it would have been too conspicuous in its habitat.

Ornithomimus comes from the Denver and Lance Formations of the very top of the Cretaceous in Colorado, and Hell Creek, Montana.

Dromiceiomimus breviterius (21)

Dromiceiomimus differs from other ostrich dinosaurs in the size of its eyes which were the largest of any land living animal. This dinosaur lived in broadleaved woodlands and with such a highly developed sense of sight is unlikely to have been a predator on dinosaur nesting sites but instead probably preyed on small mammals and lizards living on the forest floor. There is every likelihood that it was also a twilight feeder preying on the small mammals that ventured out to feed once the light fell. The discovery of an adult together with two young individuals provides a certain amount of evidence supporting the idea that the ostrich dinosaurs cared for their young in much the same way that the modern flightless birds do. The young stayed with the adults for protection even though they fed themselves.

Dromiceiomimus is known from the Edmonton Formation of the Upper Cretaceous near Trochu in the Red Deer River area of Alberta, Canada.

Struthiomimus altus (22)

Struthiomimus is one of the few dinosaurs that had a description based, in the first instance, on a perfect skeleton. Although in 1914 it was originally named *Ornithomimus*, a few years later (1917) it was given the new name of *Struthiomimus* or ostrich mimic. Subsequently most dinosaur experts believed that they were the same and the name reverted back to *Ornithomimus*. In 1972 D. A. Russell re-examined this question and came to the conclusion that they were, after all, different and so *Struthiomimus* became the correct name once again. *Struthiomimus* had much stronger forelimbs than *Ornithomimus* and lived at a different time, its remains occurring in older rocks. Furthermore *Struthiomimus* seems to have inhabited a different environment, feeding in the more open country along river banks with a vegetation of small shrubs.

Struthiomimus comes from the Oldman (Belly River) Formation and Edmonton Formation of the Upper Cretaceous, in the Red Deer River area of Alberta, Canada.

Gallimimus bullatus (23)

The largest of all the ostrich dinosaurs *Gallimimus* was described from Mongolia in 1972 and in life was 4m (13ft) in length. The hands do not seem to have been well adapted for grasping objects, unless both were used together. The fingers seem to have been particularly suited for scraping away soil or earth and this tends to support the idea that they fed on the eggs of other dinosaurs, after first uncovering them. A reconstruction of part of the skeleton is on display in the British Museum (Natural History) in London, with the backbone sloping down at about 45 degrees in much the same manner as the early reconstruction of *Tyrannosaurus*. This posture is quite inaccurate and contrasts with the model life restoration which shows the correct posture. This is one of the curious instances where the actual bones on display give a wrong impression of the animal and the artist's restoration gives the correct one.

Gallimimus comes from the Nemegt Formation of the Upper Cretaceous from Tsagau Khusu, Nemegt Basin, Mongolia.

Oviraptor philoceratops

Oviraptor philoceratops carries a name which purports to describe its way of life, as it means the 'ceratops-loving egg stealer'. This particular ostrich dinosaur was only half the size of *Ornithomimus* and was discovered in association with a nest of *Protoceratops* eggs in Mongolia.

Segnosauria

SEGNOSAURIDAE
A new division of the theropods, the Segnosauria, was established in 1980, following the discovery of several new types of carnivorous dinosaur from Mongolia. This material was described by R. Barsbold and A. Perle of the Department of Palaeontology and Stratigraphy of the Geological Institute of the Mongolian Academy of Sciences, Ulan Bator, Mongolia. The new specimens are of exceptional interest as they will necessitate a revision of the ideas previously held regarding the way in which dinosaurs have been classified. It will not be necessary to change completely the classification as now used, but there will have to be some extensive modifications.

Barsbold in 1979 announced the discovery of lightly built flesh-eating dinosaurs with a pelvic girdle in which the pubis was orientated

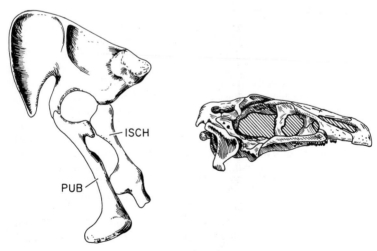

Pelvic girdle of *Segnosaurus galbinensis* and skull of *Erlikosaurus andrewsi* (after R. Barsbold and A. Perle).

I The probable coloration of the dinosaurs can be determined from knowledge of their habitats and life-styles, and by comparison with present-day animals. *Tsintaosaurus* lived in broadleaf woodland and the combination of green and brown would have camouflaged it, the large patches of colour breaking up the outline and the white undersurface reducing the effect of shadow. (See Appendix.)

II Excavation of a skeleton of the tyrannosaur *Tarbosaurus* by the Polish-Mongolian Expedition to the Gobi Desert.

III Excavation of a complete skeleton of the carnosaur *Yangchuanosaurus* in Szechuan, China.

IV Excavation of the ankylosaur *Saichania* by the Polish-Mongolian Expedition to the Gobi Desert.

V Mounted skeleton of the largest known duck-billed dinosaur *Shantungosaurus*, in the Natural History Museum, Peking, with part of the skeleton of the sauropod *Mamenchisaurus* in the foreground.

VI Lower jaw of the tyrannosaur *Tarbosaurus* in the laboratory of the Palaeobiology Institute of the Polish Academy of Sciences, Warsaw.

VII Professor Zofia Kielan-Jaworowska uncovering a nest of dinosaur eggs in the Gobi Desert.

VIII Impression of *Iguanodon* skin on a block of Wealden sandstone from Sussex, England.

IX Fossil tracks of small carnivorous dinosaurs (coelurosaurs) from Australia.

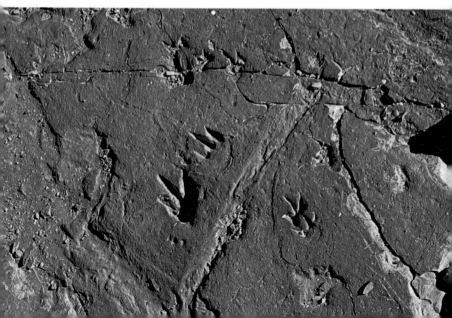

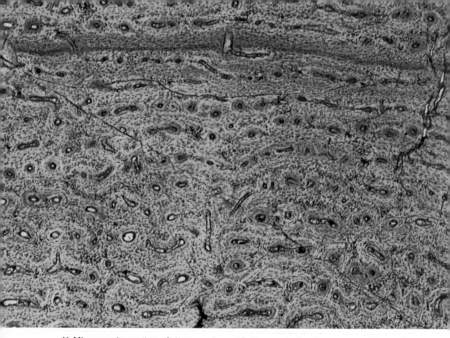

X Microscopic section of dinosaur bone (*Cetiosaurus*) showing cross-sections of blood vessels arranged in parallel rows to give a laminar structure. The small dark specks are bone cells.

XI Microscopic section of dinosaur bone (*Cetiosaurus*) showing the formation of Haversian systems of bone cylinders with central blood vessels. This type of bone allows bone renewal to take place.

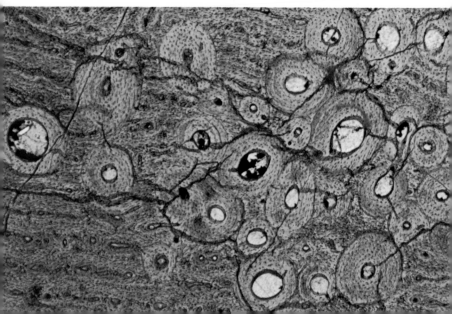

Theropoda (1-23)

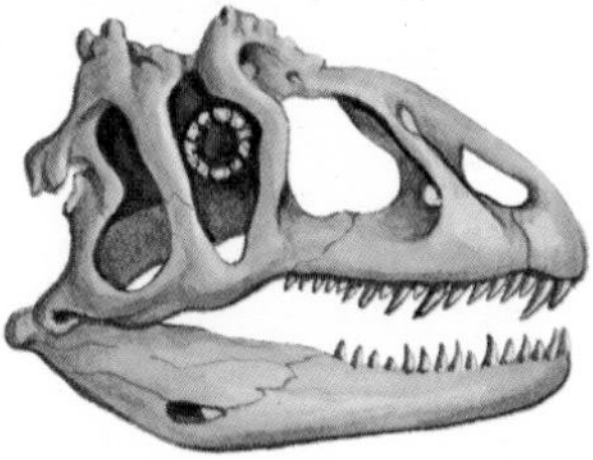

4a

1. *Ornithosuchus*
1a. Ornithosuchid skull
   (*Ornithosuchus*)
2. *Yangchuanosaurus*
3. *Megalosaurus*
4a. Megalosaur skull
   (*Allosaurus*)

2

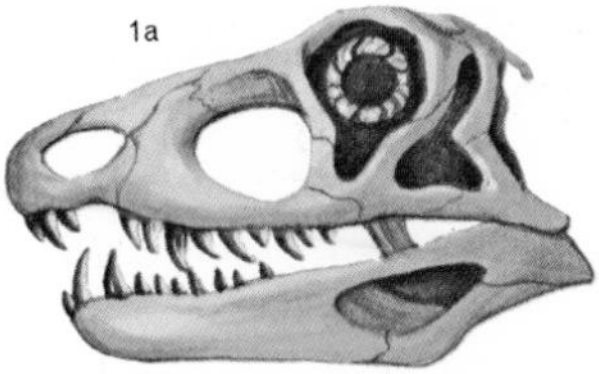

1

1a

3

1 m

4. *Allosaurus*
5. *Ceratosaurus*
6. *Dilophosaurus*
7. *Spinosaurus*

6

7

1m

8a

8. *Tyrannosaurus*
8a. Tyrannosaur skull *(Tyrannosaurus)*

8

1 m

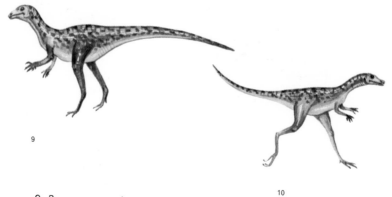

9. *Procompsognathus*
10. *Saltopus*

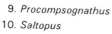

13a

13

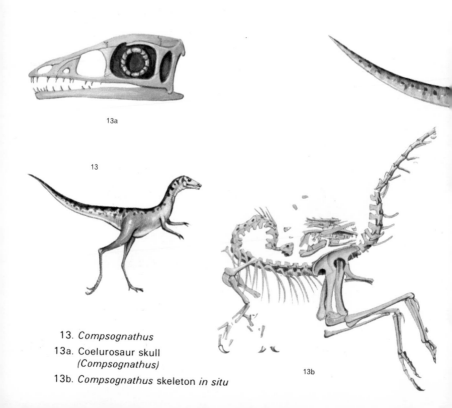

13. *Compsognathus*
13a. Coelurosaur skull
    (*Compsognathus*)
13b. *Compsognathus* skeleton *in situ*

13b

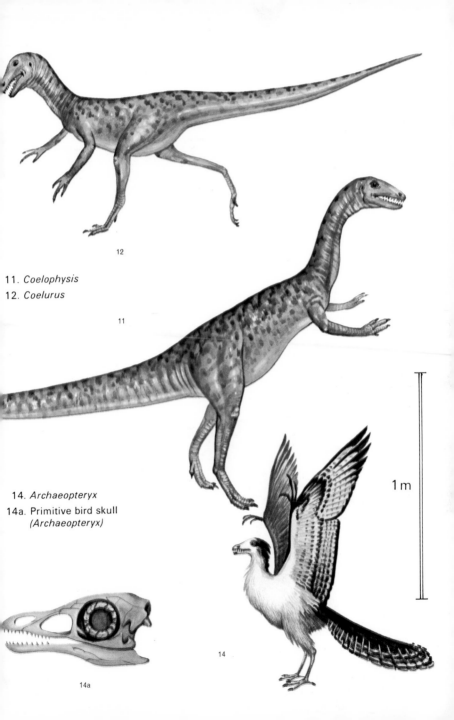

11. *Coelophysis*
12. *Coelurus*

14. *Archaeopteryx*
14a. Primitive bird skull
     (Archaeopteryx)

1 m

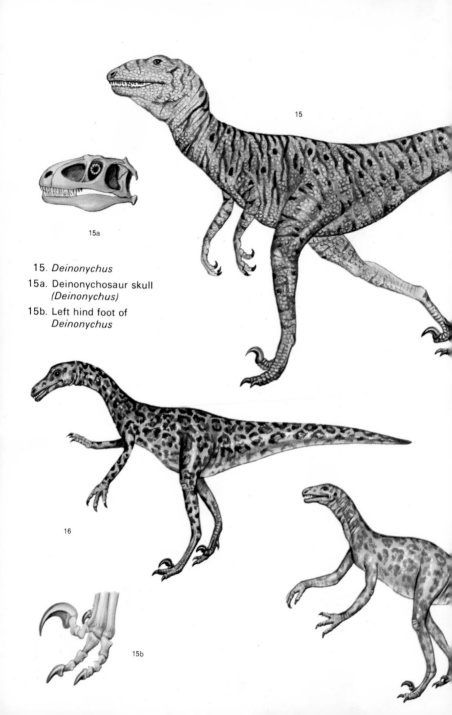

15. *Deinonychus*
15a. Deinonychosaur skull
     (Deinonychus)
15b. Left hind foot of
     Deinonychus

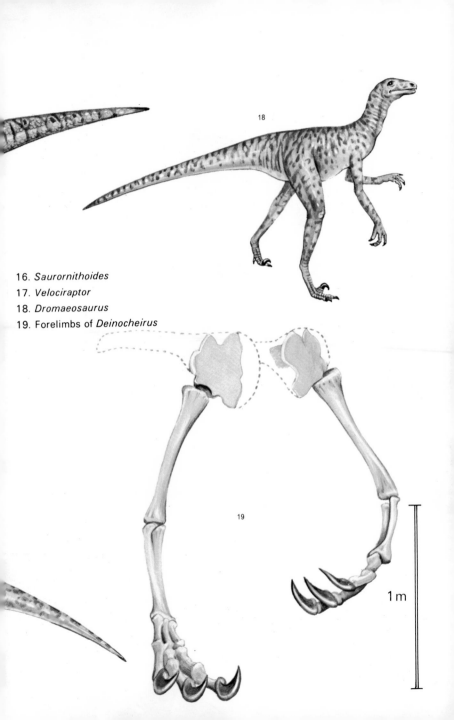

16. *Saurornithoides*
17. *Velociraptor*
18. *Dromaeosaurus*
19. Forelimbs of *Deinocheirus*

1 m

20. *Ornithomimus*
20a. Ornithomimosaur skull
(Ornithomimus)
21. *Dromiceiomimus*

22. *Struthiomimus*
23. *Gallimimus*

1 m

Sauropodomorpha (24-40)

24. *Lufengosaurus*
25. *Plateosaurus*
25a. Prosauropod skull
      (Plateosaurus)

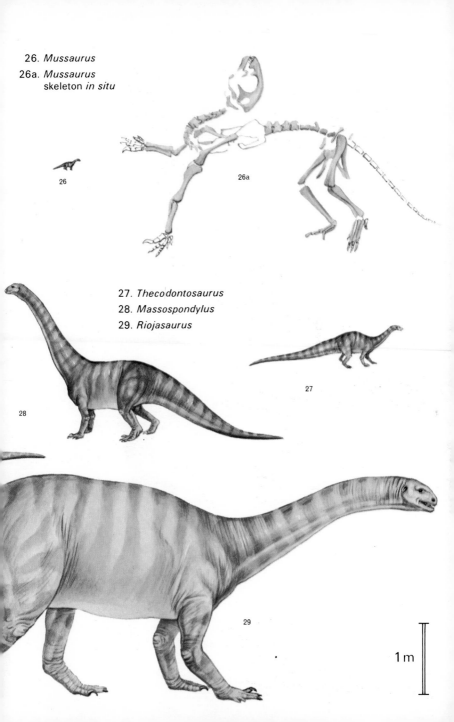

26. *Mussaurus*
26a. *Mussaurus* skeleton *in situ*

26

26a

27. *Thecodontosaurus*
28. *Massospondylus*
29. *Riojasaurus*

28

27

29

1 m

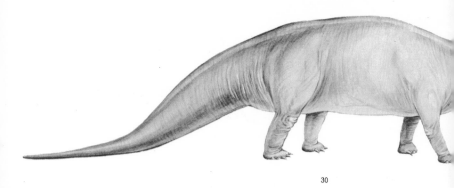

30

31

30. *Mamenchisaurus*
31. *Apatosaurus*
32. *Dicraeosaurus*
33. *Diplodocus*
33a. Atlantosaur skull
     (Diplodocus)

32

1 m

33a

33

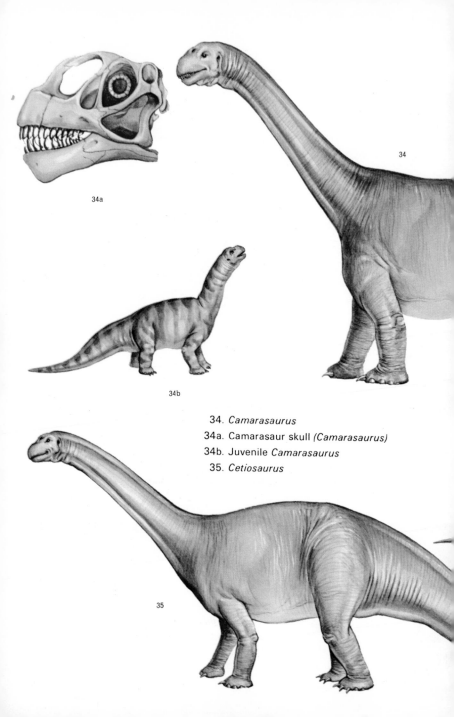

34. *Camarasaurus*
34a. Camarasaur skull *(Camarasaurus)*
34b. Juvenile *Camarasaurus*
35. *Cetiosaurus*

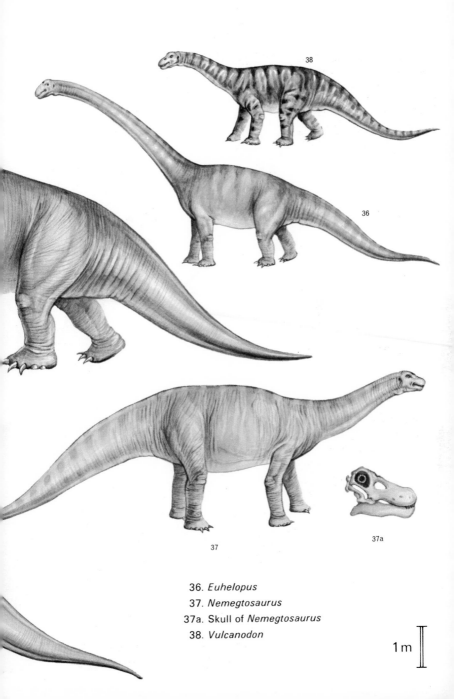

36. *Euhelopus*
37. *Nemegtosaurus*
37a. Skull of *Nemegtosaurus*
38. *Vulcanodon*

1m

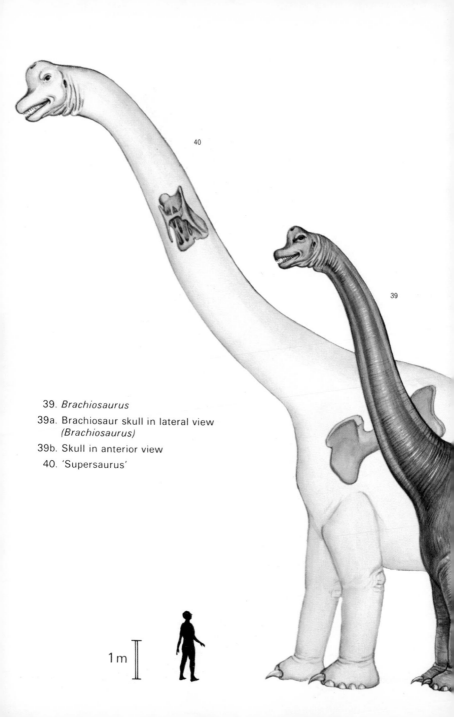

39. *Brachiosaurus*
39a. Brachiosaur skull in lateral view
     (Brachiosaurus)
39b. Skull in anterior view
 40. 'Supersaurus'

1 m

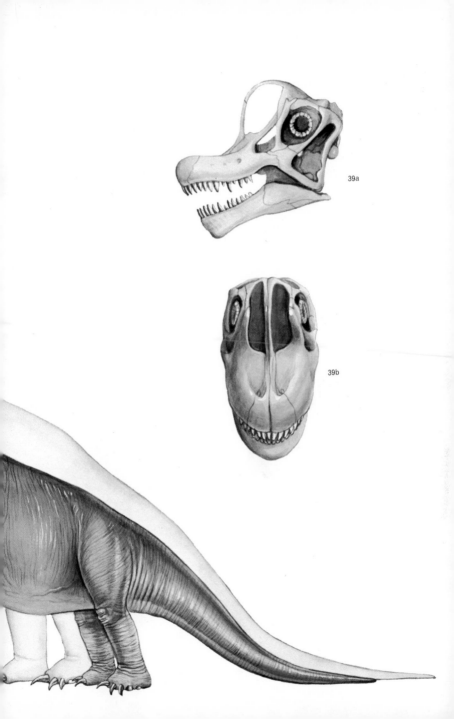

39a

39b

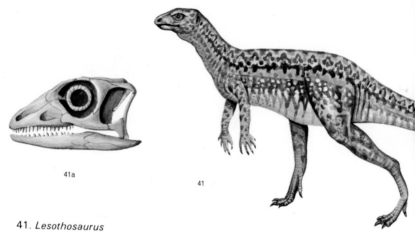

41. *Lesothosaurus*
41a. Lesothosaur skull
    (Lesothosaurus)

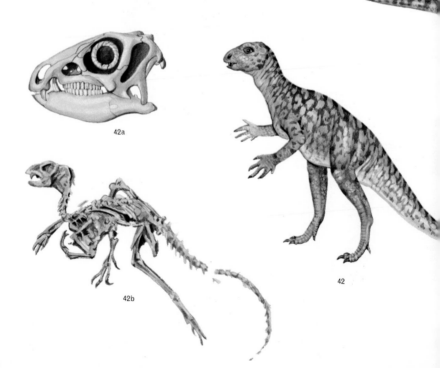

42. *Heterodontosaurus*
42a. Heterodontosaur skull
    (Heterodontosaurus)
42b. *Heterodontosaurus* skeleton
    in situ
43. *Hypsilophodon*
44. *Parksosaurus*

1 m

45

45a

45b

46

47

45. *Camptosaurus* — bipedal posture

45a. Iguanodont skull
     (Camptosaurus)

45b. *Camptosaurus* —
     quadrupedal posture

46. *Ouranosaurus*

47. *Tenontosaurus*

48. *Iguanodon*

48a. Iguanodont skull
     (Iguanodon)

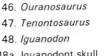

48a

48

1 m

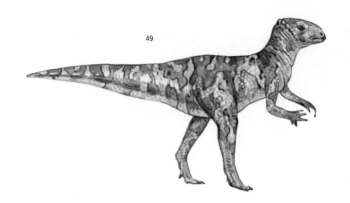

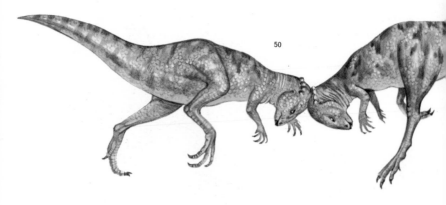

49. *Homalocephale*
50. *Stegoceras*
51. *Yaverlandia*
52. *Micropachycephalosaurus*

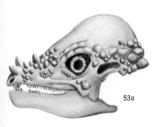

53. *Pachycephalosaurus*
53a. Pachycephalosaur skull
   (Pachycephalosaurus)

53a

53

1 m

54. *Anatosaurus*
55. *Edmontosaurus*
55a. Flat-headed hadrosaur skull
    (Edmontosaurus)
56. *Hadrosaurus*

54

55

55a

59

57. *Shantungosaurus*
58. *Brachylophosaurus*
59. *Prosaurolophus*

56

60. *Saurolophus*
61. *Maiasaura*

57

58

60

1 m

61

62. *Procheneosaurus*
63. *Cheneosaurus*
64. *Corythosaurus bicristatus*

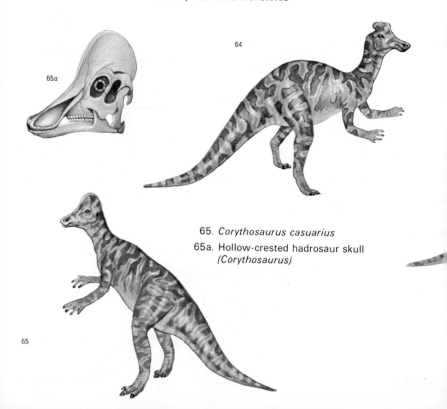

65. *Corythosaurus casuarius*
65a. Hollow-crested hadrosaur skull
     (Corythosaurus)

66. *Hypacrosaurus*
67. *Lambeosaurus lambei*

68. *Lambeosaurus magnicristatus*
69. *Parasaurolophus walkeri*
70. *Parasaurolophus cyrtocristatus*

1 m

Ceratopsia (71-86)

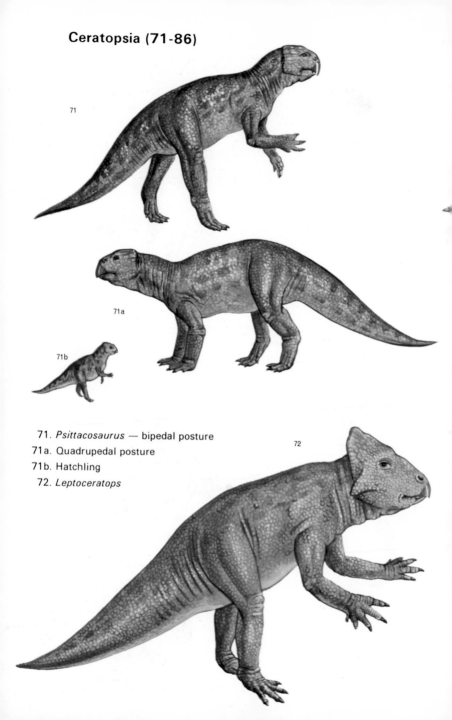

71. *Psittacosaurus* — bipedal posture
71a. Quadrupedal posture
71b. Hatchling
72. *Leptoceratops*

1 m

73. *Protoceratops*
73a. Protoceratopsian skull in lateral view *(Protoceratops)*
73b. Skull in dorsal view

74. *Bagaceratops*
75. *Microceratops*

76. *Styracosaurus*
77. *Montanoceratops*
78. *Brachyceratops*
79. *Monoclonius*

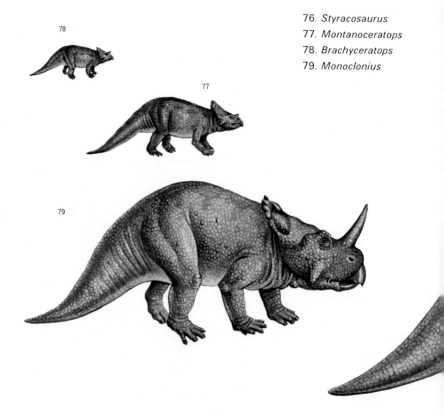

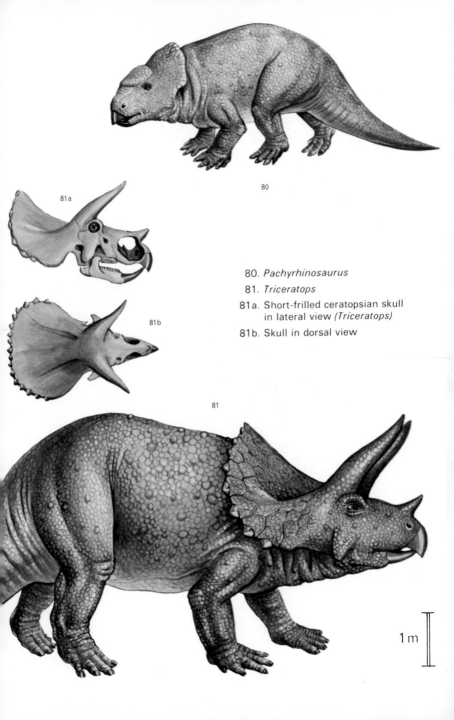

80. *Pachyrhinosaurus*
81. *Triceratops*
81a. Short-frilled ceratopsian skull in lateral view *(Triceratops)*
81b. Skull in dorsal view

1 m

82. *Chasmosaurus*
83. *Arrhinoceratops*
84. *Anchiceratops*

82

83

84

85. *Pentaceratops*
86. *Torosaurus*
86a. Long-frilled ceratopsian
   skull *(Torosaurus)*

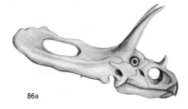

86a

1 m

Ankylosauria (87-96)

87. *Scelidosaurus*
88. *Acanthopholis*
89. *Struthiosaurus*
90. *Polacanthus*
91. *Silvisaurus*
92. Advanced ankylosaur skull
    (Panoplosaurus)

92

87

88

89

90

91

1 m

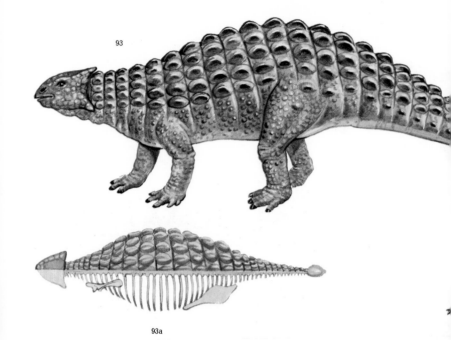

93. *Ankylosaurus*
93a. *Ankylosaurus* armour and
    skeleton in dorsal view
 94. *Scolosaurus*

95. *Palaeoscincus*
96. *Nodosaurus*

95

1 m

96

99a

98

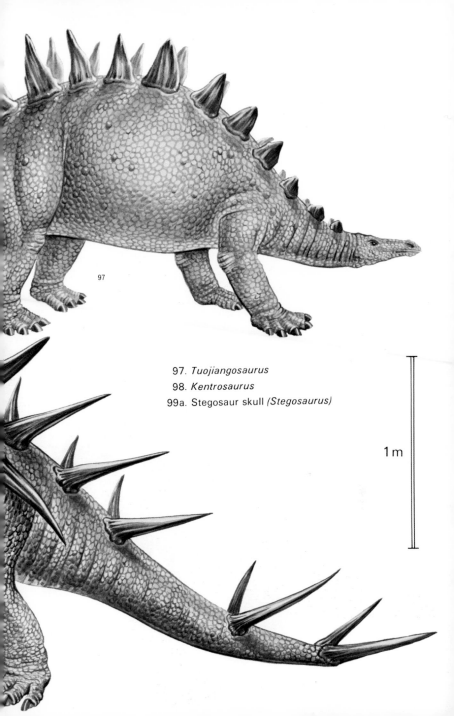

97. *Tuojiangosaurus*
98. *Kentrosaurus*
99a. Stegosaur skull *(Stegosaurus)*

1 m

1 m

99. *Stegosaurus*

parallel to the ischium and in one new form was actually fused to it. There is no question that these carnivorous dinosaurs belong to the Saurischia, which have always been recognised by the fact that the pubis pointed forwards at a large angle from the ischium.

As well as the unusual nature of the pelvic girdle, there were other distinguishing features of the skeleton: the lightly built skull was devoid of teeth at the front of the jaw; the foot possessed four toes each with a long claw and all of which pointed forwards. The segnosaurids are not yet adequately known and their relationship to the other advanced theropods is still not clear. This group clearly filled a different ecological niche from that occupied by either the ostrich dinosaurs or the clawed dinosaurs. Barsbold and Perle tentatively suggested that they may have been semiaquatic and preyed on fish. Until new data becomes available there is no way of deciding the matter, although the dentition and structure of the foot would seem to militate against a fish-eating mode of life.

Segnosaurus galbinensis

The first description of this dinosaur was published in 1979 in the Results of the Soviet-Mongolian Palaeontological Expedition by A Perle. The remains consisted of a lower jaw which was toothless anteriorly with 24 to 25 small teeth in the posterior part. Bones of the fore and hind limbs were preserved together with parts of the vertebral column and the pelvic girdle. The limb girdle is unique among theropod dinosaurs, indeed among all saurischians, by virtue of the orientation of the pubis which pointed backwards and was aligned parallel to the ischium. The anterior part of the ilium was developed into a characteristic expansion. On the basis of this specimen Barsbold and Perle recognised the existence of a new and previously unsuspected major type of theropod dinosaur.

Segnosaurus comes from the Bayan Shireh horizon of the Upper Cretaceous of Amtgay, South East Mongolia.

Erlikosaurus andrewsi

This dinosaur was smaller in size than *Segnosaurus* and is based on a reasonably complete skull and lower jaw together with the feet. The name is derived from the name of the Lamaist deity Erlik, the king of the dead. The skull shows the striking reduction of the teeth, the front of the jaws being completely toothless. The lower jaw and other parts are similar to *Segnosaurus*.

Erlikosaurus comes from the Bayan Shireh horizon of the Upper Cretaceous of Baysheen Tsav, South East Mongolia.

5
Sauropodomorpha – Reptile-Footed Dinosaurs

The Sauropodomorpha are the second major division of the Saurischia, which are all characterised by the typical reptilian pelvis in which the pubis is directed forwards. There is a ledge on the ilium above the limb articulation and the region where the three bones meet is opened out to form a window or fenestra. In fact the limb girdle is astonishingly similar to that of the bipedal carnivorous Theropoda. With the exception of perhaps a few of the early members, the sauropodomorphs were heavily built quadrupedal dinosaurs. Without exception all had small heads and long necks. Most had peglike teeth although some of the earliest forms had small serrated teeth which were indistinguishable from those of the primitive Triassic carnosaurs. The sauropodomorphs fall into two groups: the primitive prosauropods which are restricted to the Triassic and the more advanced sauropods or brontosaurs which include the largest land animals of all time.

Prosauropoda

The prosauropods represent one of the most significant stages in the evolution of the dinosaurs. The most primitive members showed a marked difference in the respective lengths of the fore and hind limbs and it is evident that they were capable of walking on their hind limbs but as they increased in size they became entirely quadrupedal. But perhaps the major change is seen in the nature of the teeth. The numerous small serrated teeth were the same as those of the contemporary small carnivores and it seems likely that like them they were originally carnivorous. The large body, long neck and small head suggests that they could not have been active hunters. In fact the later development among the prosauropods indicates an exclusively vegetarian diet, which means that this group made the change from a flesh-eating diet to a plant-eating mode of life.

The best known prosauropods are the plateosaurids of which many complete skeletons have been found in Germany. These illustrate the typical small skull and moderately long neck and tail. The dinosaurs included in this family were about 6m (20ft) in length. The pelvic girdle was clearly primitive as there were only three sacral vertebrae to which the girdle was attached. The hands show several striking features which are the trademark of the prosauropods as a whole. The thumb was massive with a large claw, the second and third fingers were long and slender and also bore claws, but the fourth and fifth fingers were reduced and did not have any claws. The hind feet had four clawed toes and the fifth was reduced.

Lufengosaurus huenei (24)

Lufengosaurus was named after F. von Huene who provided the authoritative study on *Plateosaurus*. *Lufengosaurus* was a marginally more lightly built version that was discovered in China and is important in that it illustrates the world-wide success of the prosauropods.

Lufengosaurus comes from the Lower Lufeng Series, of the Uppermost Triassic, in Yunnan, China.

Plateosaurus quenstedti (25)

Plateosaurus was the subject of an exhaustive study by von Huene in 1928, based on large numbers of complete skeletons preserved in a desert sandstone. Two mounted skeletons are on display in the Palaeontological Institute of the University of Tübingen, Germany, one standing on its hind limbs, the other on all fours, emphasising the ability of the prosauropods to be either bipeds or quadrupeds. As well as the detailed description of the anatomy of *Plateosaurus* von Huene made a special study of the habitat in which the remains were preserved. It seems that a zone of desert separated a moister hilly region from the shores of an inland sea and von Huene postulated that with the onset of the dry season the plateosaurs migrated in large herds across this desert, which was about 120km (75 miles) wide, to reach the more favourable conditions near the shoreline of the large inland sea. During the course of this migration which he considered took two or three days the weaker and juvenile individuals must frequently have perished and the wind blown sands would have later covered their skeletons, thus preserving them.

Plateosaurus comes from the Keuper Sandstones of the Upper Triassic, of Trossingen, Germany.

MUSSAURIDAE

Mussaurus patagonicus (26)

Mussaurus or mouse reptile was described from Argentina in 1979. The largest specimen was only 200mm (8in) in length and such a tiny dinosaur clearly merited being designated the mouse of the dinosaurs. However, this dinosaur was a very young individual and was found with some five others and the remains of two eggs all associated in a nest. This was important as it showed that after hatching the young remained together in the nest. The features of the skull are a little reminiscent of the later sauropods, but the extreme shortness of the neck vertebrae seem to be similar to the ancestors of the dinosaurs, the thecodonts, and it was because of these differences from other prosauropods that Bonaparte and Vince created the new name for this tiniest of the dinosaurs.

Mussaurus comes from the El Tranquilo Formation of the Colorada Series of the Upper Triassic of Laguna La Colorada, Santa Cruz Province, Patagonia, Argentina.

THECODONTOSAURIDAE

The thecodontosaurs were similar to the plateosaurs except that they were about half the size and were more lightly built. Their teeth were identical to those of carnivorous dinosaurs. The thecodontosaurs probably represented the basal stock of the prosauropods.

Thecodontosaurus antiquus (27)

The bones and the teeth of *Thecodontosaurus* were first discovered mixed up with angular fragments of Carboniferous Limestone held together by a fine grained yellow marly silt. This breccia, as such rocks are termed, had been formed from the collapse of the roof of an ancient cave. Bones of various dinosaurs, or rather isolated bones of dinosaurs, lying on the surface, fell in amongst the angular limestone blocks and others were probably washed in. Among the rolled and broken bones were occasional tiny skeletons of lizards which must have wandered into the hollow and died there. The discovery of dinosaur remains associated with what would have been hilly country at the time the caves were formed, is important evidence regarding the kind of environment that *Thecodontosaurus* inhabited.

Thecodontosaurus comes from the Dolomitic Conglomerate of the Upper Triassic of Durdham Down in the City of Bristol, Avon, and from the Lower Keuper Sandstones of Warwickshire and Worcestershire.

Yaleosaurus colurus
Yaleosaurus from the Red Sandstones, Upper Triassic, of Connecticut and Massachusetts is a form hardly distinguishable from *Thecodontosaurus*. This dinosaur formerly known as *Anchisaurus* has the distinction of being the first dinosaur to be recognised in North America.

Massospondylus carinatus (28)
Massospondylus from the Upper Red Beds of the Stornberg Series of the Upper Triassic of South Africa is a further prosauropod which is included with *Thecodontosaurus* but differs from it essentially in its size, being about 4m (13ft) in length. Its presence in southern Africa further extends the geographical range of the prosauropods.

MELANOSAURIDAE
The melanosaurids are separated from the plateosaurs basically by their large size. These prosauropods were significantly larger than *Plateosaurus* reaching 12m (40ft) in length, double the length of *Plateosaurus*. The dimensions of the melanosaurs has led to the speculation that they were the prosauropods that were directly ancestral to the sauropods. Unfortunately the structure of the hands and feet shows that they were simply giant prosauropods and not the first of the true sauropods. In the deposits in South Africa which have produced the remains of *Melanosaurus* there are trackways that were made by a genuine sauropod. To date none of its bones have been found but it can be safely stated that the sauropods were already in existence by the end of the Triassic period.

Riojasaurus incertus (29)
The discovery of *Riojasaurus* from the Upper Triassic rocks of Patagonia in South America established that this type of giant prosauropod was not confined to southern Africa. This distribution is not too surprising since at the time Africa and South America were united and there would have been little hindrance for land animals to move from one place to the other. The features of *Riojasaurus* which suggest a closeness to the sauropods are the solid bones of the limbs in conjunction with the excavated cavernous vertebrae. Bone seems only to have formed along the major lines of stress. This type of vertebra combines the greatest strength with the minimum weight and was an adaptation to cope with the increase in weight of these advanced prosauropods.

Sauropoda
The sauropods, popularly known as brontosaurs, are the very essence

of what is recognised as a dinosaur. They had four pillar-like limbs, extraordinarily long necks with small skulls and long whip-like tails. The feet were broad and spreading. On the hand the thumb bore a large claw. The other fingers were reduced and clawless. On the hind foot the first three toes had claws and the fourth and fifth were without. The limb bones were constructed of solid bone whereas the vertebrae were excavated so that they looked more like pieces of engineering scaffolding, which is in effect what they were. The traditional view of these dinosaurs is that they were very slow, clumsy, ponderous animals and recent studies of their footprints have confirmed that this was indeed the case. The speed at which they walked was only about 4kph ($2\frac{1}{2}$mph) and if they had been able to reach 12kph ($7\frac{1}{2}$mph) the forces acting on the bones would have fractured them. It has even been demonstrated that they were unable to bend their limbs more than about 45 degrees, again because the forces to which they would have been subjected would have broken them. As well as being so huge, the largest weighing about 100 tonnes, the evidence of footprints shows that even such colossi lived in herds. They also seem to have had some kind of social structure in that, when they were on the move, the smaller individuals travelled in the centre of the group and in this way would have been protected from the attentions of large flesh-eating dinosaurs. Although the latter were, in the main, scavengers they could undoubtedly have despatched with ease any young brontosaur that had become detached from the herd.

The generally held view was that these dinosaurs spent much of their life in the shallow waters of lakes and swamps. There have been suggestions put forward recently that they were fully land dwelling and used their long necks in the manner of giraffes to feed off foliage at the tops of trees. The peglike teeth seem to be singularly inappropriate for such a method of feeding and most probably were used to rake in soft plant material, along the margins of swamps and lakes.

A famous footprint trackway from North America shows a brontosaur swimming – this is proved by the fact that the track is made up of prints of the hands only, except at the point where it changed direction. At this point one of the hind limbs was brought down to stick in the river or lake bed, the body swivelled round and the handprints then continued as the dinosaur pawed its way along the bottom in a new direction. These footprints provide graphic evidence of the swimming ability of the sauropods and go a long way to confirm the view that the brontosaurs were essentially semiaquatic. In one respect, however, they were like all the other reptiles – they laid their eggs on land.

The sauropods are of many different kinds and they are classified into five separate families – the mamenchisaurs, atlantosaurs, camarasaurs, barapasaurs and brachiosaurs.

MAMENCHISAURIDAE
Mamenchisaurus hochuanensis (30)

Mamenchisaurus constructus was described sometime ago from China but in 1972 a fairly complete skeleton was described and it possessed such curious specialisations that it was placed in a new family of its own. The reconstructed skeleton is now on display in the Natural History Museum in Peking. By far the most sensational aspect of this dinosaur is the length of its neck – it had by far the longest neck of any animal that has ever lived. Although it might appear that this neck was almost snake-like, in fact in life it must have been fairly rigid. The ribs of the neck vertebrae developed long bony projections running backwards so that each of these ribs overlapped three vertebrae. In effect the neck was additionally strengthened by these extra rods of bone which must have restricted any untoward bending. However these rods were not developed near the head so that the end of the neck was clearly flexible. The structure of the neck means that it was habitually held in a horizontal position and hence *Mamenchisaurus* could in no way have fed off the tops of high trees but it could easily have allowed its neck to float in this position and to sweep around with its head collecting up aquatic plants.

Mamenchisaurus comes from Upper Jurassic rocks in Szechuan, China.

ATLANTOSAURIDAE

The atlantosaurids include the most familiar of the sauropods – *Brontosaurus* properly called *Apatosaurus,* and *Diplodocus.* In all the members of this family the hind limbs are markedly longer than the forelimbs so that the back slopes forward from the hips to the shoulders. The tail is whip-like and the skull has a sloping face. The nostrils open on the top of the head in the midline just in front of the eyes and the peg-like teeth are restricted to the front of the mouth.

Apatosaurus ajax (31)

Apatosaurus was based on a fairly complete skeleton and later the name *Brontosaurus* was introduced for dinosaur material which was found to be the same as *Apatosaurus.* This means that the correct name is *Apatosaurus* but the name *Brontosaurus* or 'thunder lizard' is so well known and evocative that it is still used as the general colloquial name for all sauropods. *Apatosaurus* has mounted skeletons on display in several American Museums and in these and in all published restorations the head is short and deep quite unlike that of the other atlantosaurids. This is due to the fact that the skull on display in fact belonged to a quite different type of dinosaur – a camarasaur. It was not until 1979 that a genuine *Apatosaurus* skull was discovered and it was then realised that in life it had a much longer skull. *Apatosaurus* is the archetypal dinosaur and in life weighed about 30 tonnes.

Apatosaurus comes from the Morrison Formation of the Upper Jurassic in Jefferson County, Colorado.

Dicraeosaurus hansemanni (32)

Dicraeosaurus is one of the smaller members of the atlantosaurs. It was only 13m (43ft) in length, the neck was only moderately long and the tail, although drawn out, was hardly whip-like. The skull, however, was of the typically atlantosaurid type with the characteristic sloping face. A complete mounted skeleton is on display in the Palaeontological Museum of Humbold University in Berlin and was part of the major collection made, between 1909 and 1912, at Tendaguru in what was then German East Africa, now Tanzania. In 1907 a fund-raising committee was set up to finance a major excavation and collected £25,000 ($50,000) which was a fortune at that time. The bone quarries which were opened employed 500 labourers and during the first three years 4300 loads of fossil bones were packed off on the heads and backs of native carriers to the coast. Altogether some 200 tonnes of fossil bones were shipped back to Berlin from East Africa. W. Janesch began a series of monumental studies on the dinosaurs of Tendaguru beginning before World War 1 and continuing into the 1950s. Curiously, among the devastation that Berlin suffered at the end of World War 2, when the museum was damaged, the materials that came through unscathed were the dinosaurs of Tendaguru.

Dicraeosaurus comes from the Upper Jurassic of Tendaguru, Tanzania.

Diplodocus carnegii (33)

The skeleton of *Diplodocus* has been seen by more people in the world than any other dinosaur. This dinosaur was the longest with an exceptionally long whip-like tail and long neck, yet for all its impressive length weighed a mere 10 tonnes when alive, a third of the weight of *Apatosaurus*. The reason that *Diplodocus* is the best known is that casts of its skeleton are on display in most of the world's major museums. The story behind this fact is worth telling.

At the beginning of the century, in 1902, E. Douglas joined the staff of the Carnegie Museum in Pittsburgh and began a notable career as a dinosaur collector. He discovered an important deposit of articulated dinosaur remains in Utah and, with the financial backing of Andrew Carnegie the steel millionaire, a vast collection of dinosaurs was amassed. An almost perfect complete skeleton of a *Diplodocus* was extracted and was described in a major monograph by W. J. Holland and named *Diplodocus carnegii* in honour of Andrew Carnegie. The skeleton was put on display in the Carnegie Museum in Pittsburgh but Carnegie was so pleased at having such a splendid skeleton named after him that he felt it should be able to be seen by many other people in the world, who might never get to Pittsburgh. He asked Holland who was the Museum's director to have casts made, so that they could be distributed to major museums throughout the world. Accordingly Holland went to Serafini Augustini, who sold religious medallions in a nearby shop and also produced plaster casts of statues of saints, to set about casting the 300 bones of *Diplodocus*. Eventually ten complete sets were completed and Holland supervised the setting up of these gifts from Andrew Carnegie in the British Museum (Natural History) in London, and museums in Paris, Frankfurt, Bologna, Berlin, Vienna and La Plata in the Argentine.

There is one curious postscript to this story. When the original skeleton was found the front feet were missing and so replicas of the hind feet were placed on the front legs. The hind feet of all the sauropods bear three claws and the front feet of the museum skeleton of *Diplodocus* also bear three claws. Unfortunately the front feet of all sauropods including *Diplodocus* have only one claw on the thumb and none on any of the other fingers. But because everyone has seen the skeleton of *Diplodocus*, the majority of pictures of the life appearance of *Diplodocus* and all other sauropods show three claws on the front feet.

Diplodocus comes from the Morrison Formation of the Upper Jurassic from the Green River, near Vernal, Utah. (This fossiliferous region is now included in the Dinosaur National Monument.)

The first knowledge of *Diplodocus* in Europe came in 1977 when A. Hutt discovered new remains on the Isle of Wight, England.

CAMARASAURIDAE

The camarasaurs contrast with the atlantosaurs by being more compact. They did not have such long tails and the difference between the fore and hind limbs was not so pronounced. The shoulder region

117

was usually high so that the back sloped from the shoulder down to the hip, the exact opposite of the atlantosaur condition. The other feature that distinguished the camarasaurs was the skull, which was short and deep, rising to a peak in front of the eyes. Furthermore the massive teeth were not restricted just to the front of the mouth and the nostrils opened on the top of the head at the summit of the skull.

Camarasaurus supremus (34)

Camarasaurus is the dinosaur on which the camarasaurs were distinguished from other sauropods. Although the forelimb was in fact shorter than the hind limb the shoulder was considerably higher so that the back had its characteristic slope which seemed to be going the wrong way, compared with the more familiar sauropods. The head was comparatively large for a sauropod and was particularly notable for the inflated nasal region. The nostril opened at the top of the head and this is the usual sign of a water-dwelling air breather. Most of the body and head could be submerged with just the nostrils protruding above the waterline. The nasal region, as well as being flared, showed that the internal surface area of the nasal organ must have been greatly enlarged and this would have provided an important cooling organ by evaporation from the lining. This arrangement would have helped to lower the temperature of the brain during the heat of the day. The main body temperature of the dinosaurs, even those only 1m in section, hardly fluctuated more than 1 or 2°C. The surface-to-volume ratio ensured that the internal temperature remained the same. However, the temperature at the skin must have varied as much as the air temperature and so overheating of structures near the surface could have been a problem and the one organ that was in just such a dangerous situation was the brain. The provision of increased evaporative surfaces by the enlargement of the nasal apparatus would have overcome these problems.

Camarasaurus is one of the few sauropods in which the skeleton of the young is known. A skeleton of an individual 5m (16ft) in length was discovered in Utah and this shows the differences in bodily proportions between juvenile and adult dinosaurs. The head was comparatively larger and the neck and tail very much shorter. The length of the neck clearly increased at a greater rate than the rest of the body.

Camarasaurus comes from the Morrison Formation of the Upper Jurassic, in Colorado, Oklahoma, Utah and Wyoming.

Cetiosaurus oxoniensis (X, XI, 35)

Remains of *Cetiosaurus* were the first of a sauropod to be discovered, beginning with the find of a tail vertebra at Dorchester-on-Thames, Oxfordshire in 1809. When W. Buckland gave the first description of *Megalosaurus* in 1824 he mentioned the existence of huge bones that had been found near Enslow Bridge, Oxfordshire, which he thought may have belonged to either whales or crocodiles. For many years no-one could decide to what sort of animal the huge limb bones and vertebrae belonged. In 1841 Richard Owen described them as *Cetiosaurus* meaning 'whale reptile', and he came to the conclusion that they belonged to an aquatic reptile that must have been a crocodile. That same year he introduced the new concept of the dinosaur, in fact he invented the name then, but he did not recognise that *Cetiosaurus* was another member of his Dinosauria. It was not until the more complete remains of sauropods were discovered from North America that it was possible for *Cetiosaurus* to be included among them. The structure of the limbs suggest that *Cetiosaurus* belonged to the camarasaurs.

Cetiosaurus comes from Middle and Upper Jurassic rocks in Oxfordshire, England.

Euhelopus zdanskyi (36)
Euhelopus is a camarasaur which is notable for its elongated neck. The forelimbs were sufficiently long for this dinosaur to have the typical camarasaur sloping back. The skull was proportionately longer than typical members of this family and seemed to approach the overall shape of *Diplodocus*. However, the large inflated nasal organ opening on the top of the head was constructed to the same pattern as *Camarasaurus* and so there is no doubt about its relationship to the camarasaurs.

Euhelopus comes from the Lower Cretaceous rocks of Shantung Province, China.

Nemegtosaurus mongoliensis (37)
Nemegtosaurus was based on a skull that was described in 1972. It was fairly high but with the sloping face of the atlantosaurs as well as the teeth being restricted to the front of the mouth. Similarly the nasal apparatus was comparable to that in the atlantosaurs. In 1977 a skeleton from the same geological horizon was described but there was no head and even the neck was missing. The details of the vertebrae and limb bones established that this skeleton was a camarasaur and it was named *Opisthocoelicaudia*. In view of this it would seem reasonable to postulate that it also had a relatively short neck like most of the other camarasaurs. The real question is whether the skull belongs to the skeleton or not. The simplest way of resolving the

matter is just to accept that there were two different kinds of sauropod in the deposit and one lost its body and the other its head. If it is believed that they belong to the same dinosaur then a serious problem arises: here would be a dinosaur with an atlantosaur head and camarasaur body, which seems unlikely. However there are other examples of dinosaurs which seem to combine characteristics of more than one kind and so such a solution is not completely out of the question. For the moment, therefore, it is provisionally accepted, until more evidence comes to light, that the two should be combined and that this composite dinosaur should carry the name *Nemegtosaurus*.

Nemegtosaurus comes from the Nemegt Formation of the Upper Cretaceous of the Nemegt Basin, Mongolia.

Vulcanodon karibaensis (38)
In 1972 the remains of part of a skeleton of a new dinosaur were described. These had come from a lens of sandstone sandwiched between two lava flows. The teeth were similar to those of the early prosauropods – they were small with serrated edges; but of much greater significance the rest of the skeleton, especially the limb bones, indicated that it was a sauropod. The slope of the back seemed to indicate that it was closer to the camarasaurs than the atlantosaurs and, for this reason, it has been included very provisionally as a possible beginning of the camarasaur line. The other possibility is that it is a very advanced member of the melanosaur prosauropods.

Vulcanodon comes from a sandstone near the base of the Stromberg volcanic succession of Lower Jurassic age, from an unnamed island in Lake Kariba, Zimbabwe.

BARAPASAURIDAE
Barapasaurus tagorei
Barapasaurus is the first undoubted sauropod in the fossil record and is known from numerous bones which accumulated in a kind of bone log-jam. This dinosaur still retained a few prosauropod features but in all essentials was a true sauropod. It is not possible to assign it to either the atlantosaurs or the camarasaurs and although a skeletal reconstruction has been mounted in the Geological Museum of the Indian Statistical Institute, Calcutta, there is insufficient evidence to determine the actual length of either the neck or the tail. There are, however, a number of skeletal features in the vertebrae which seem to be unique, such as large cavities on the inside of the dorsal spines of the vertebrae and also depressions on the sides of the vertebral bodies. These two features separate *Barapasaurus* from the other

sauropods and suggest that it should be placed in a family of its own.

Barapasaurus comes from the Kota Formation, Gondwana Group, of the Lower Jurassic from the village of Pochampali, Chanda district, Maharastra, India.

BRACHIOSAURIDAE

The brachiosaurs were by far the most sensational of the sauropods and indeed of all the dinosaurs as they have the distinction of including the largest land animals of all time. In contrast to all other dinosaurs the forelimbs were longer than the hind. The slope of the back, from the shoulder to the hip, was very strongly marked. The beginning of this tendency was seen in the camarasaurs which are generally united with the brachiosaurs. The basic structure of the skull is very similar in that the nasal apparatus is strikingly expanded to open at the very summit of the head. The fact that the forelimbs are clearly longer than the hind is sufficient reason to separate the brachiosaurs and place them in their own independent family.

Brachiosaurus brancai (39)

Brachiosaurus was first described from the Upper Jurassic of Colorado but the best known skeleton comes from Tendaguru, Tanzania, from where it was excavated before World War 1. A complete mounted skeleton is on display in the Palaeontological Museum of Humbolt University, Berlin, and is one of the most dramatic dinosaur reconstructions imaginable. The head towers 12m (40ft) above the ground and the length is 23m (75ft). The fact that the nostril is at the very top has led to the suggestion that it lived in fairly deep water with its head stretching up to the surface to breathe. In fact it has been calculated that this mode of existence would have been impossible because the water pressure at such depth would have collapsed the lungs and crushed the blood vessels in the neck. It is much more likely that the head and neck were held out more or less horizontally from the shoulder region in much the same manner as all the other sauropods. This does not mean that *Brachiosaurus* was not capable of raising its neck and head as in the posture of the Berlin skeleton. It most assuredly could have done so. Recently it has been suggested that *Brachiosaurus* was a land dweller feeding off the tops of trees in the manner of a giraffe but the effort involved in obtaining sufficient food from such a method of feeding seems rather unlikely, especially as such animals lived in groups. A swamp dwelling existence seems by far to have been the most likely environment for such enormous animals.

Brachiosaurus comes from the Tendaguru Formation of the Upper Jurassic of Tendaguru, Tanzania.

'Supersaurus' (40)

In 1971 in the Dry Mesa Quarry in western Colorado, J. Jensen discovered the remains of a further brachiosaur. This skeleton has not been fully excavated but several bones have been collected. The size of this particular dinosaur is so huge that it has been christened 'Supersaurus'. So far it has not been described and has not been given a scientific name. If this 'Supersaurus' were of the same general build as *Brachiosaurus* then from the bones so far extracted, such as a single neck vertebra the length of a man, it must have been able to reach at least 15m (50ft) and would have been nearly 30m (100ft) long. A rough calculation of its weight indicates a weight of 100 tonnes, as much as the large ocean-going whales. The discovery of 'Supersaurus' has effectively settled one of the recent controversies regarding the physiology of large dinosaurs. Some years ago it was argued that the dinosaurs were warm blooded in the same sense as birds and mammals, which maintain a constant high internal temperature by consuming and burning up large amounts of food. This is known as having a high metabolic rate. Living reptiles on the other hand depend on the external temperatures and their food requirements are relatively small. They maintain their temperature at a fairly constant level by sunning themselves when they are cool and seeking the shade when it is too hot. Dinosaurs had a constant internal temperature simply by being large – their surface area compared to their volume was so small that they were incapable of either warming up or cooling down rapidly. It is likely that they avoided overheating by living partly in water. A large bull elephant, which is warm blooded, eats between 130 and 270kg (290–600lb) per day to fuel itself and has to spend up to 18 hours a day feeding. 'Supersaurus' weighed the equivalent of 15 large elephants and if its energy requirements were the equivalent of large mammals' their food consumption would have been many more times that of an elephant and it would have been a physical impossibility for them to have consumed a great enough volume of food within a period of 24 hours for a single day's needs. This means simply that the sauropods could not have been warm blooded in the same sense as birds and mammals but that their energy requirements were essentially of the reptilian kind.

6
Ornithopoda – Bird-Footed Dinosaurs

This group are named ornithopods because of their somewhat bird like feet, which bore either blunt claws or hooves. The longest toe was the third with the second and fourth being shorter, the first and fifth were either greatly reduced or missing altogether. There were two basic types of ornithopods – a group of small lightly built forms and a series of more heavily built types. The essentially lightly built ornithopods include the most primitive of all the ornithischians, the lesothosaurs, the heterodontosaurs and the hypsilophodonts. The larger ornithopods include the iguanodonts, the boneheads or pachycephalosaurs and finally the most advanced of all the herbivorous dinosaurs, the duck-billed dinosaurs or hadrosaurs.

LESOTHOSAURIDAE
Lesothosaurus australis (41)
The early history of the ornithischians was almost a blank until the 1970s when R. A. Thulborn described the skull and skeleton of *Lesothosaurus*, which was a small running herbivore. The details of its skeleton showed that it was by far the most primitive ornithischian known. The pubis was turned so that it was parallel to the ischium but there was no prepubic process developed as in all the later ornithischians. The other feature which was the most primitive condition of the ornithischians was in the skull. There was no sign of the concave cheek region which means that the characteristic cheek pouches had not yet developed in *Lesothosaurus*.

One of the most interesting aspects of the life of *Lesothosaurus* was that during the hot dry season when food would have been difficult to obtain they aestivated – that is the hot season equivalent of hibernation which many mammals undergo when the climate gets cold in the winter. Living crocodiles bury themselves in muds at the onset of the dry season in South America, Asia and Africa and they sleep for several months, only waking up when the conditions improve and abundant food is once more available. The conditions in which *Lesothosaurus* lived suggest that aestivation would have been an advantageous method of coping with the annual drought. There is evidence that *Lesothosaurus* did aestivate. Two small individuals were found together, and it is known that crocodiles often aestivate together, but the conclusive evidence was that the teeth in the jaws were newly erupted while near them were the remains of shed worn teeth. There were no other kinds of remains around. While the dinosaurs were sleeping during the summer months, their teeth were gradually being replaced in the normal reptilian manner, the old worn ones were shed and the new ones erupted. This process takes place over many weeks and this association can only be explained if the two individuals concerned had remained in the same spot over a few months. Unfortunately they died before they were due to wake up and remained buried in the holes they had previously dug.

The name *Lesothosaurus* means the Lesotho reptile but when these remains were described they were called *Fabrosaurus* as they were thought to belong to the same kind of reptile that had been named *Fabrosaurus* on the basis of a small piece of jaw bone. Some scientists still insist on calling this dinosaur *Fabrosaurus* but to avoid any confusion it is better to use the name *Lesothosaurus* as this form is based on adequate material.

Lesothosaurus comes from the Red Beds of the Stormberg Series of the Upper Triassic of the Likhoele Mountain, near Mafeteng, Lesotho.

HETERODONTOSAURIDAE
Heterodontosaurus tucki (42)
Heterodontosaurus was first described from a single skull in which there were different kinds of teeth, hence the name which means 'the differentiated toothed reptile'. *Heterodontosaurus* had small grasping incisor-like teeth at the front of the jaw, canine-like tusks further back and behind these were ridged grinding teeth. This type of dentition was very mammal-like and completely different from that in any previously known reptile. This was a remarkable discovery and it was hard to understand why the earliest known ornithischian, as it was when first found, should have had such a specialised dentition. As well as grinding its food it also possessed muscular cheeks, a feature which characterised the later ornithischians. When the later *Lesothosaurus* was discovered, it was realised that *Heterodontosaurus* must have been a very early evolutionary sidebranch of the ornithischians.

One author has suggested that *Heterodontosaurus* should be named *Lychorhinus* because a part of a jaw which now seems to be the same had been described under this name as long ago as 1924, but most scientists prefer to use the name *Heterodontosaurus* which is based on excellent remains. In 1976 a complete skeleton was described with the result that the anatomy of this dinosaur is now very well known. In its pelvic girdle the pubis was the same as in *Lesothosaurus* establishing that, in spite of its specialised dentition, it was a very primitive ornithischian.

Heterodontosaurus comes from the Cave Sandstone of the Upper Triassic of Herschel District, Cape Province, South Africa.

Heterodontosaurus consors

In 1974 a skull of a *Heterodontosaurus* was described, which was the same as the original one with one major difference: it did not have any canine-like tusks. This specimen was named *Lycorhinus consors* meaning the wife of *Lycorhinus* (the scientist in this case preferred *Lycorhinus* to *Heterodontosaurus*). Another scientist disagreed and suggested that this form was quite new and he gave it a new name *Abrictosaurus*, but in fact it was simply a *Heterodontosaurus* without tusks and in all probability was the female of the same kind. It is clear that *Heterodontosaurus* did not use its tusks for feeding, they were simply weapons or display structures in the same way as the tusks of the small Chinese water deer.

Heterodontosaurus consors comes from the Red Beds, of the Stormberg Formation of the Upper Triassic, at Noosi, near Whitehill, Lesotho.

HYPSILOPHODONTIDAE

The hypsilophodonts represent the direct descendants of the lesothosaurids and in most respects are very similar. They remained a group of primitive, lightly built ornithopods which continued with little change until the final extinction of the dinosaurs. The main advances which they showed which distinguished them from their Triassic ancestors were the development of an elongated anteriorly directed prepubic process in the pelvic girdle and in the formation of muscular cheek pouches.

Hypsilophodon foxii (43)

Hypsilophodon was first described in 1870 by T. H. Huxley, although Mantell had, in 1849, described some bones of this same form as belonging to a young specimen of *Iguanodon*. There have been many studies of this particular skeleton and it was believed that it was possibly a tree dweller and numerous restorations show it perched up in the branches of trees. The idea that *Hypsilophodon* was a tree dweller was first put forward in 1882 and most authors agreed with this as they believed that the first toe pointed backwards and so could have enabled the dinosaur to perch in the same way as birds. A completely new study was published in 1974 by P. M. Galton and he showed conclusively that the first toe was not opposable, that in fact *Hypsilophodon* was incapable of climbing and perching but was really a fast runner confined to the ground.

Hypsilophodon comes from the Wealden Marls, Wealden, Lower Cretaceous, of the Isle of Wight, England.

Parksosaurus warreni (44)

Parksosaurus is one of the last representatives of the hypsilophodonts from the Upper Cretaceous and is known from the left half of a skeleton. Presumably when it died it sank into the sediment, lying on its left side, the bones of the right side were then broken up and eroded away before they could be buried.

Parksosaurus comes from the Edmonton Formation, Upper Cretaceous, of the Red Deer River area, Alberta, Canada.

Thescelosaurus neglectus

Thescelosaurus is a more massively constructed member of the hypsilophodonts, which some authors place in the more advanced iguanodonts. The femur is longer than the tibia and in this regard it differs from the normal hypsilophodonts but like them it retains teeth in the anterior part of the upper jaw, which is a primitive condition and allies this dinosaur with *Hypsilophodon*.

Thescelosaurus comes from the Lance Formation, Upper Cretaceous, of Wyoming.

IGUANODONTIDAE

The main evolution of the ornithischians was an increase in size. From the small lightly built 1m long lesothosaurids there developed the heavily built iguanodonts, which reached 8m (26ft) in length. In the main these dinosaurs were still bipedal when on the move but when feeding would have been on all fours. The main change that took place in the skull was the loss of the teeth from the front of the upper jaw so that there was a cropping horny beak present on both upper and lower jaws. The preorbital fenestra in front of the eyes became progressively smaller while the nostrils became greatly enlarged. It has been thought that this indicated that the salt gland came to be associated directly with the nasal apparatus.

Camptosaurus dispar (45)

The earliest and most primitive member of the iguanodonts was the 7m (23ft) long *Camptosaurus*. The very first example of this, *Camptosaurus prestwichi*, was found in the Upper Jurassic Kimmeridge Clay of Oxfordshire, although it was originally identified as *Iguanodon* and only restudied in 1980 by P. M. Galton and H. P. Powell. As it came from Cumnor it was later named *Cumnoria* but is now recognised as belonging to *Camptosaurus*, which was named earlier and based on fairly complete skeletons.

In *Camptosaurus* the preorbital fenestra is greatly reduced and the foot has small hooves on the first four toes although the first is much smaller than the others. In all the later iguanodonts there are only three functional toes with hooves on the hind foot. *Camptosaurus* is a primitive generalised heavy iguanodont and can be considered as the ancestor of all the later types.

Camptosaurus comes from the Morrison Formation of the Upper Jurassic of Wyoming.

Ouranosaurus nigeriensis (46)

In 1966 a complete skeleton was collected from the Sahara desert and ten years later was fully described as a new type of iguanodont and named *Ouranosaurus* by P. Taquet. The skeleton was on display in Paris but is now in the National Museum in Niamey, Niger. The shape of the skull differs from the normal iguanodonts in having a flat top, which forms an angle with the sloping face. The most surprising feature of *Ouranosaurus* was the greatly elongated dorsal spines of the vertebrae, which must have supported a large sail over the main part of the back. *Ouranosaurus* lived on the open flood plain of a large river inhabited by giant crocodiles, as well as other dinosaurs, and this sail would have acted as an important cooling organ enabling this dinosaur to prevent overheating in such open country.

Ouranosaurus comes from the Gadoufaoua deposit of the Aptian, Lower Cretaceous, at Gadoufaoua in the Tenere desert, Sahara, Niger.

Tenontosaurus tilletti (47)

Tenontosaurus was a descendant of *Camptosaurus* which seems to have become much more of a quadruped with a much longer tail than the usual iguanodonts. Perhaps this dinosaur's major claim to fame is in the manner of its death. Its remains are associated with those of about five individuals of the sickle clawed *Deinonychus*, which suggests that it had been attacked by a pack of these flesh-eaters.

Tenontosaurus comes from Cloverly Formation, Lower Cretaceous, of Montana.

Iguanodon mantelli (VIII, 48)

Since the beginning of the last century there have been many more discoveries of *Iguanodon*, from Maidstone in Kent and the Isle of Wight in particular. In the Wealden sandstones *Iguanodon* footprints are known, which confirm that *Iguanodon* habitually walked on its hind feet. There is even the impression of the skin where an individual sat down on the damp sand (Plate VIII). From extensive studies of the rocks in which *Iguanodon* occurs, it has been established that southern England was a wide flat lowland area across which braided streams flowed and where vast meadows of horsetails or scouring rushes grew. From the severe wear on the teeth of *Iguanodon*, it seems that this was the main diet of these dinosaurs.

Iguanodon was first discovered in the Tilgate Stone, part of the Wadhurst Clay of the Wealden, Lower Cretaceous, at Cuckfield, Sussex, England.

Iguanodon bernissartensis

One of the most exciting dinosaur discoveries took place in 1878 when a group of Belgian coal miners suddenly encountered sand full of bones instead of coal. This was the site of an ancient valley that had been cut into the Coal Measures at the time of the dinosaurs. Mining stopped and, under the direction of Louis Dollo, the bones were carefully excavated. Some 30 complete skeletons were extracted and many of these are now on display in the Brussels Natural History Museum, some exactly as they were preserved and others mounted in life positions. This particular find provided the conclusive evidence with regard to the posture of *Iguanodon* and showed that the 'nasal horn' belonged on the thumb. However, the other major conclusion that was drawn from this discovery was that these giant 8m (26ft) long plant-eating dinosaurs must have lived in herds. Not only that but there were differences between the males and females in their overall proportions. It is assumed that the smaller and rather more lightly built individuals were the females and the more robust the males. In spite of *Iguanodon* being so familiar it is only recently that a comprehensive monographic study of this dinosaur has been undertaken by D. Norman, whose results were published in 1980.

PACHYCEPHALOSAURIDAE

During the Cretaceous period a group of curiously specialised dinosaurs evolved from the hypsilophodonts. These were the pachycephalosaurs or bone-heads. The tops of their heads were formed of thick masses of bone and were ornamented by fringes of bony tubercles. The bony thickening was not spongy but was of compact bone with fibrous columns oriented perpendicularly to the outer surface. Such an arrangement of the tissue would seem to be adapted for resisting a force applied to the top of the head. Furthermore, there are structures in the neck which helped to resist any lateral bending. The only possible function that can be imagined for such a bony thickening would be to act as battering rams. As such they would not have been particularly effective against predators and so it seems much more likely that they were used against one another, in exactly the same way that sheep and goats crash their heads together in combat today.

This mode of behaviour therefore implies that the males indulged in trials of strength and that they lived in groups, each with a dominant male. As with sheep and goats both males and females possessed structures suitable for use as battering rams, and the stronger and more effective ones belonged to the males. The type of behaviour envisaged for the boneheads has its parallel among many living tropical lizards which spend a large proportion of their time engaged in combats among their own kind.

The bone-heads were first described from North America in 1902 from the Upper Cretaceous but it was not until the 1970s that they were described from many other parts of the world. The ancestral bone-head comes from the Lower Cretaceous of the Isle of Wight, and in 1974 several new forms were described from Mongolia, in 1978 from China and in 1979 from the Malagasy Republic (Madagascar).

Homalocephale calathoceros (49)
The most complete skeleton of a pachycephalosaur belongs to *Homalocephale*, which has a rather flattened top to its skull although it bears the characteristic ornamentation of a row of bony tubercles across the back of the skull and along the side of the head. One of the curious features of the skeleton occurs in the pelvis, which is loosely connected to the vertebral column. This may well be connected with absorbing the shock that ensued when they used their heads as battering rams. The way in which the pelvic region widened posteriorly suggests that there was a particularly wide abdomen and has led to the suggestion that these bone-heads may have given birth to live young. The pelvic girdle flares out posteriorly and this specialisation is not found in other groups of dinosaurs.

Homalocephale comes from the Nemegt Formation, of the Upper Cretaceous, of Nemegt Basin, Mongolia.

Stegoceras validus (50)

Stegoceras, which was only about 2m (6½ft) in length, shows a number of features which link it with the hypsilophodonts, such as the presence of teeth in the front of the upper jaw. The top of the skull forms a smooth rounded dome some 50mm (2in) thick with a frill of small bony tubercles along the back of the skull. The females seem to have had smoother domes. In Alberta in the main geological formation from which the bone-heads have been found, they make up nearly 8% of the dinosaur fauna. *Stegoceras* remains consist, in the main, of fragments of thickened skull roofs, which have been severely water worn. Remains of other parts of the skeleton are exceedingly rare. It is evident that after the dinosaurs had died their bones were washed by streams and rivers to be deposited in the flood plains inhabited by different dinosaurs. It is clear that *Stegoceras* must have lived long distances from the places where their water worn bones have been found and it is generally considered that they lived in upland or hilly regions and not in the same environment as the majority of other dinosaurs. This is especially likely as they do not seem to have been particularly agile and, apart from their bony domes, were utterly defenceless.

Stegoceras comes from the Oldman Formation (Belly River Formation) of the Upper Cretaceous of Alberta.

Yaverlandia bitholus (51)

Yaverlandia, from the Isle of Wight, is considered to be the ancestral form of the bone-heads. Although it is only known from the top of a skull of an individual less than a metre long, it demonstrates clearly the characteristic thickening. This suggests that the use of the head as a battering ram as postulated for the typical bone-heads had already begun in *Yaverlandia*. *Yaverlandia* is the oldest bone-head so far known and from its size must have been similar to its contemporary *Hypsilophodon*. It may well be that the change in behavioural pattern marked the initial divergence of the bone-heads from the hypsilophodonts.

Yaverlandia comes from the Wealden Marls of the Wealden Lower Cretaceous of Yaverland, Sandown, Isle of Wight, England.

Micropachycephalosaurus hongtuyanensis (52)

In 1978 remains of a minute dinosaur about half the size of *Yaverlandia* were identified as a new bone-head *Micropachycephalosaurus*. It is difficult to be certain whether this dinosaur was a hypsilophodont or a pachycephalosaur as the pelvic girdle does not seem to flare out in the typical manner of the bone-heads. However, on balance it seems reasonable to accept the provisional identification as a small pachycephalosaur.

Micropachycephalosaurus comes from the Wang Formation, Campanian, Upper Cretaceous, Laiyang, Shantung, China.

Pachycephalosaurus grangeri (53)
Pachycephalosaurus was the last of the bone-heads and by far the largest, being of much the same size as the heavily built iguanodonts but with a wider pelvic region. The thickening of the top of the skull reached its extreme, being 250mm (10in) thick. The development of spiky bony tubercles on the skull also reached its most exaggerated condition. As well as bony spikes forming a frill at the back of the skull, they were also developed above the tiny nostrils on the front of the snout.

Pachycephalosaurus comes from the Lance Formation, Upper Cretaceous, Montana. Closely related forms also occur in Wyoming and South Dakota.

Majungatholus atopus
The first record of a pachycephalosaur from any of the southern continents was made in 1979 when the thickened skull roof of a new form named *Majungatholus* was described. Although much younger in age it was remarkably similar to *Yaverlandia* and represents a surviving member of the primitive bone-heads. It was probably about twice the size of *Yaverlandia* being about 1.4m ($4\frac{1}{2}$ft) in length.

Majungatholus comes from the Mavarano Sands, Campanian, Upper Cretaceous, from the Majunga District of north west Malagasy.

HADROSAURIDAE
The hadrosaurs or duck-billed dinosaurs represented the peak of the evolution of the bipedal herbivores. They experienced one of the major evolutionary radiations of all the dinosaurs and for a time must have been by far the most successful and well adapted of all the plant-eating dinosaurs, making up about 75% of the fauna. The hadrosaurs originated from iguanodonts rather like *Camptosaurus* and are notable in that the skeletons are virtually indistinguishable from one form to another. The tails were more flattened from side to side than in other dinosaurs. The feet had three toes which bore hooves, the first and fifth toes having been lost. On the hands the thumb was missing, the second and third fingers bore small hooves, the fourth had no hoof nor had the smaller slender fifth finger. The feature which gives these dinosaurs their popular name is the flattening of the front of the snout and its expansion to form a duck-like bill. The

131

edge of the predentary bone at the front of the lower jaw had rough crenulations and this was used to crop plants against the upper duck-bill. The dentition also showed important specialisations. There were several longitudinal rows of teeth in each jaw, between 45 and 60 vertical rows each with about 6 successional teeth one above the other, giving a total of between 1600 and 2000 teeth in the jaws. In the lower jaw there were three longitudinal rows and in the upper two. The inner margin of the lower teeth and the outer of the upper had a layer of highly mineralised enamel. As the two tessellated pavements of the wear surfaces dragged across each other during chewing, the differential hardness of the enamel and the softer dentine ensured the maintenance of sharp ridges which served to grind up tough plant material, in exactly the same way that horses and cows grind up their food. The development of muscular cheeks would also have helped in the general chewing process. The hadrosaurs represent one of the few herbivorous dinosaurs which provide direct evidence of their diet. In a number of specimens there are plant remains preserved in their stomachs and these consist of pine needles, twigs and pine cones. This confirms the view derived from a study of the teeth and jaw apparatus that the hadrosaurs were capable of coping with exceedingly tough plant material.

The other part of the head which showed a series of striking developments was the nasal apparatus. The more primitive hadrosaurs had flat heads but the nasal openings were enormously expanded and elongated, which means that the inner surface area of the nasal organs must have been greatly increased. In the more advanced hadrosaurs the bone at the tip of the upper jaw, the premaxilla, and the nasal bones were themselves expanded to produce large hollow crests on the top of the skull, through which the nasal passages passed. There have been many theories regarding the significance of this tremendous increase in the surface area of the lining of the nasal passages. There are three possible explanations, which are not mutually exclusive. Indeed it is likely that all three are correct. The increase in the lining of the nasal cavity must have significantly increased the sensitivity of the sense of smell. For a herbivore that had no obvious means of defence an acute sense of smell would have been a key factor in survival, warning the individuals of the approach of danger. A recent idea that has been suggested is that these large passages acted as resonating chambers, allowing the hadrosaurs to roar and bellow across the landscape to one another. Crocodiles are known to be particularly noisy, especially during the mating season, when they bellow and roar in what is sometimes described as a growling rumble.

The most recent view is that the increased nasal passages provided a large evaporative area allowing excess heat to be lost so that the temperature of the brain could be kept the same as the deeper levels of the body tissues. In the hadrosaurs there was a space just behind the eye where a large blood sinus, the orbital sinus, was situated and this in conjunction with the evaporative surface area of the nasal passages could have served effectively as a cooling device for the brain.

By far the most ludicrous interpretation that has been put forward in all seriousness is that the spaces acted as a kind of combustion chamber which allowed the hadrosaurs to belch out fire and smoke to ward off over-attentive predators. The 'evidence' for this idea is supposedly contained in the Bible (the book of Job ch. 41, v. 19–21) in which the 'Behemoth' is described as having 'firebrands shoot from his mouth . . . his nostrils pour forth smoke'. In the *New English Bible* Behemoth is translated as crocodile. For many centuries, travellers described the crocodile as having clouds of smoke pouring from its mouth ('Clouds of smoke issued from his dilated nostrils', Bartram, 1791 quoted in *The Travels of William Bartram*, ed. M. van Doren, 1928, New York). In fact crocodiles emit vapoury jets of musk from glands on their chins and this must indeed have seemed like smoke to the early travellers and could well have given rise to the idea of fire-breathing dragons. It is ironic that this misinterpreted piece of early natural history observation should in the 1970s have been taken literally and been proposed as an explanation of the crests of the duck-billed dinosaurs.

There has been a further less unusual interpretation of the significance of the head crests and that is that they were display structures and served as recognition signals among members of the same species.

The hadrosaurs are among the few dinosaurs in which there is evidence of the texture of their skin. Many mummified specimens are known so that the details of their skins can be portrayed with a high degree of accuracy. Similarly it is known that they lived in a variety of habitats – some in dark swampy cypress forests, others in open woodland of broadleaved trees and yet others along the flood plains of large meandering rivers with a low shrub-like vegetation. It seems unlikely therefore that the colour patterns of forms inhabiting these different environments would have been the same. It is probable that they would have had colour patterns that would have served to camouflage them in the particular conditions in which they flourished.

One of the most important finds of hadrosaurs was described in 1979 from Montana. It comprised a nest mound within which were 11 immature hadrosaurs each about a metre long. Their teeth were worn and they were all partly grown so they had not just hatched from the eggs. This discovery established that dinosaur nurseries existed and that the young hadrosaurs continued to live together after they had hatched. The fact that they lived in a wide saucer-like depression situated on the top of a large mound 3m (10ft) in diameter and 1.5m (5ft) high would have made their presence extremely conspicuous and would undoubtedly have attracted the attention of the flesh-eating predators. Such exposed habitats could only have succeeded and the vulnerable young survived, if there had been some kind of parental protection. This is therefore the first really conclusive evidence that dinosaur parents protected their offspring.

The hadrosaurs are known from early Cretaceous rocks in Mongolia with the form *Batractosaurus*. This is based on a complete skeleton but unfortunately the head is missing. From rocks of the same age near Cambridge, England, a single hadrosaur tooth has been found but nothing much can said about it beyond the fact that it proves that the hadrosaurs had a wide distribution. The main evolution of the hadrosaurs has been documented from North America and eastern Asia, in Mongolia and China. The hadrosaurs achieved their greatest evolutionary developments towards the end of the Cretaceous period in the Oldman Formation and then went into a decline; their numbers fell dramatically and only a few types managed to continue through to the very end of the Cretaceous, when with all the other surviving dinosaurs they met their final extinction.

Anatosaurus annectens (54)

Anatosaurus or 'duck reptile' was one of the last survivors of the dinosaurs. The skull was relatively long and flat with the typical duck-like bill. The interesting feature of this particular dinosaur is that it was one of the most primitive members of the hadrosaurs. Other species of *Anatosaurus* were present earlier in the history of the group and as with other groups of animals the early and more primitive types often outlasted their more highly specialised relatives.

Anatosaurus annectens comes from the Lance Formation, Upper Cretaceous, of Wyoming.

Edmontosaurus regalis (55)

Edmontosaurus is very similar to the early species of *Anatosaurus*. However, the skull is comparatively shorter and higher so that the slope of the face is a little steeper. It is probable that *Edmontosaurus* was the ancestor of *Anatosaurus*. Recent studies have shown that *Edmontosaurus* lived in dark swampy cypress forests.

Edmontosaurus comes from the Edmonton Formation, Upper Cretaceous, of the Red Deer River, Alberta, Canada.

Hadrosaurus navajovius (56)

Hadrosaurus was the first dinosaur to be recognised as being bipedal. Joseph Leidy, in 1858, described the partial skeleton of a dinosaur which he named *Hadrosaurus foulkii*, and he considered that because of the difference in lengths of the fore and hind limbs this herbivorous reptile must have had a kangaroo-like posture. This skeleton, unfortunately missing the skull, came from the Matawan Formation of the Upper Cretaceous of New Jersey. It is curious that as far back as 1787 at a meeting of the American Philosophical Society a large thigh bone ('probably a hadrosaurus') was recorded also from New Jersey.

In 1910 a skull was described as *Kritosaurus* which was found to be the same as a further skull named *Gryposaurus* in 1914. This last skull was perfectly preserved and showed the nasal bones to have been very deep and excessively arched, so that the front part of the face appeared inflated. This type of hadrosaur is generally known as *Kritosaurus* and it is possible to trace the evolutionary history of its particular lineage through several geological formations. In 1977 in a review of this form it was concluded that *Kritosaurus* and *Hadrosaurus* could be shown to be the same when minor anatomical details of the skeleton were examined. This means that *Kritosaurus* should be renamed *Hadrosaurus*. As *Hadrosaurus* was the first duck-bill dinosaur to have been described and has given its name to the entire group, it is satisfying that its name should be accepted again in the general scheme of hadrosaur evolution.

Hadrosaurus navajovius comes from the Kirtland Formation, Upper Cretaceous of New Mexico.

Shantungosaurus giganteus (V, 57)

Shantungosaurus has the distinction of being the largest known hadrosaur. The mounted skeleton of this form is on display in the Natural History Museum, Peking (Plate V). The proportions of the skull were similar to those of *Anatosaurus* and in this regard *Shantungosaurus* could be considered as a surviving member of a primitive group of the flatheaded hadrosaurs. The striking feature of it is its significantly greater size, being over 12m (40ft) in length.

Shantungosaurus comes from the Campanian, Upper Cretaceous, of Shantung, China.

Brachylophosaurus canadensis (58)

Brachylophosaurus is the most primitive member of the hadrosaurs known as the 'solid-crested' duck-bills. In this form the nasal bones are extended over the top of the skull to produce a small crest of bone which projects as a small spike at the back of the skull. No-one has been able to suggest the reason for this curious structure and it may well have been simply a type of display decoration.

Brachylophosaurus comes from the Oldman Formation, Upper Cretaceous, of the Red Deer River, Alberta, Canada.

Prosaurolophus maximus (59)

Prosaurolophus is a further primitive member of the solid crested hadrosaurs. In this form there is a small raised crest, formed from the nasal bones, which is situated just above the anterior margin of the orbits, This dinosaur is the possible ancestor of *Saurolophus*.

Prosaurolophus comes from the Oldman (Belly River) Formation, Upper Cretaceous, Alberta, Canada.

Saurolophus angustirostris (60)

Saurolophus is one of the few hadrosaurs that are found in both Asia and North America. *Saurolophus osborni* was described in 1912 from a complete skeleton from the Edmonton Formation in Alberta, Canada. In this the nasal bone formed a large spine rising above the orbits and projecting above the level of the skull. In 1952 a further skeleton of the same general type was described from Mongolia. Again the nasal spine projected above the skull but in this instance projected well beyond the back of the head. This particular skeleton is on display in the Palaeontological Institute Museum in Moscow.

Saurolophus angustirostris comes from the Nemegt Formation, Upper Cretaceous, from Nemegt Basin, Mongolia.

Tsintaosaurus spinorhinus (I)

Tsintaosaurus is one of the more dramatic looking hadrosaurs. It clearly belongs to the same basic lineage as *Saurolophus* but instead of the nasal spike projecting in the same general direction as the line of the face, it projects at right angles and produces an elongated forward projecting spine slightly expanded at its tip, where it bifurcates. A mounted skeleton of *Tsintaosaurus* is displayed in the Museum of the Institute of Vertebrate Palaeontology and Palaeoanthropology in Peking. The life restoration is based directly on this mount.

Tsintaosaurus comes from the Wangsi Formation, Upper Cretaceous, of Hsikou, Shantung, China.

Maiasaura peeblesorum (61)

In 1979 a hadrosaur nursery was described for the first time. The nest mound, made from mud, was 3m (10ft) in diameter with a height of

1.5m (5ft) and the summit had a saucer-like depression excavated in it with a diameter of 2m (6½ft) and maximum depth of 750mm (30in). Within the nest were the remains of 11 immature hadrosaurs and outside were bones of a further four individuals. All the specimens represented partly grown juveniles about a metre in length. It was evident that the young hadrosaurs remained together long after hatching in a situation that must have made them a conspicuous landmark and thus attractive to any predator that happened to come along. The fact that this arrangement could ever have existed must mean that there was some kind of protection and this could only have been provided by the proximity of the parents. It is from this particular occurrence that it is now believed that the hadrosaurs looked after their young. The specimens of *Maiasaura* have a small bony spike developed above the orbits, pointing forwards. In this sense it is reminiscent of the greatly elongated forward pointing projection of *Tsintaosaurus*.

Maiasaura comes from the Two Medicine Formation, Campanian, Upper Cretaceous, from 20km (12 miles) west of Choteau, Montana.

Procheneosaurus praeceps (62)

Procheneosaurus (*Tetragonosaurus*) is considered to be the most primitive example of the hollow crested hadrosaurs. This dinosaur had an incipient crest developed from the premaxilla and nasal bones in which the nasal passages were expanded to form a crest raised above the orbits. The nasal passage formed an S-bend within the crest.

The name *Procheneosaurus* was erected without any species being designated and after 1931 such names were invalid. When the first species was described it was given the name *Tetragonosaurus*. This was meant to replace the invalid name *Procheneosaurus* but subsequently most authors have used the name *Procheneosaurus*. The present situation is even more complicated as some scientists consider that the different species of *Procheneosaurus* (*Tetragonosaurus*) were merely juvenile individuals of *Corythosaurus*. If this should turn out to be the case then the name *Procheneosaurus* would have to be transferred to *Corythosaurus*.

Procheneosaurus comes from the Oldman (Belly River) Formation, Upper Cretaceous, from the Red Deer River, Alberta, Canada and the Two Medicine Formation, Montana.

Cheneosaurus tolmanensis (63)

Cheneosaurus is thought to be descended from *Procheneosaurus*. There was a prominent crest composed of the premaxillae and nasals which reached its highest point in the region of the orbits. Unlike its predecessor there are no complications regarding its name. However, it has been recently suggested that this dinosaur is the juvenile of *Hypacrosaurus*. If this should be the case then, since *Hypacrosaurus* has priority, *Cheneosaurus* would have to be changed to it.

Cheneosaurus comes from the Edmonton Formation, Upper Cretaceous, from the Red Deer River, Alberta, Canada.

Corythosaurus bicristatus (64)
Corythosaurus had a large crest made up mainly of the nasal bones, which had a height almost as great as the rest of the skull. The premaxilla formed the anterior part of the crest, running along the sloping part of the face it then rose upwards at a sharp angle to form the anterior margin of the main part of the high crest, a thin process rising to the summit.

The nasal passage of *Corythosaurus bicristatus* has the S-shape as in *Procheneosaurus* but posteriorly had a further bend.

This species is notable for the sharp angle at which the crest rose in front of the orbits, the summit of the crest was somewhat iregular and more or less straight.

C. bicristatus comes from the Oldman (Belly River) Formation, Upper Cretaceous, from the Red Deer River, Alberta, Canada.

Corythosaurus casuarius (65)
The original species of *Corythosaurus* was described in 1914 and was one of the first hadrosaurs to be discovered with the skin texture preserved intact. The crest was made up mainly of the nasals which formed a high rounded helmet-like structure. The premaxillae formed the anterior margin of the crest with a thin strip of bone rising to the anterior summit. A detailed monograph on the skull of this species was published in 1961 by J. H. Ostrom. The species was the most advanced member of the *Corythosaurus* evolutionary line although it gave rise to *Hypacrosaurus*.

C. casuarius comes from the Oldman (Belly River) Formation, Upper Cretaceous, from the Red Deer River, Alberta, Canada.

Hypacrosaurus altispinus (66)
Hypacrosaurus represents a further development of the condition seen in *Corythosaurus*, in that the premaxilla now forms more than half of the crest at the expense of the nasals. Instead of merely forming the anterior edge of the crest, the premaxillae have expanded further. The posterior part of the crest was raised clear of the skull from just behind the orbits. *Hypacrosaurus* represents the last member of the *Corythosaurus* lineage.

Hypacrosaurus comes from the Edmonton Formation, Upper Cretaceous, from the Red Deer River, Alberta, Canada and from the Two Medicine Formation, Montana.

Lambeosaurus lambei (67)

Lambeosaurus was a contemporary of *Corythosaurus* but showed a still further advance on the organisation of the crests. The entire crest was composed of the expanded premaxillae so that it virtually obscured the nasal bones. As well as the rounded hollow dorsal crest there was a well marked spike which projected above and behind the skull. Even this posterior spike was made up of the premaxillae.

In *L. lambei* the nasal passages are even more complex than those of *Corythosaurus* as they have a further convolution so that the internal surface area is greater, even though the size of the crest is not as large as in *Corythosaurus casuarius*.

This species is notable for the prominence of the long posterior spike, which projects well above and behind the back of the skull. The hollow anterior part of the crest tends to slope forwards at a slight angle and in this respect contrasts markedly with species of *Corythosaurus*.

L. lambei comes from the Oldman (Belly River) Formation, Upper Cretaceous, from the Red Deer River, Alberta, Canada.

Lambeosaurus magnicristatus (68)

This species as its name implies represented the most extreme evolutionary development of *Lambeosaurus*. The posterior spine is poorly developed but the main part of the crest, again made up almost entirely of the premaxillae, was considerably larger than the rest of the skull. Not only was it huge in respect to the skull as a whole, but it projected forwards so that it almost reached as far forwards as the tip of the snout.

L. magnicristatus comes from the Oldman (Belly River) Formation, Upper Cretaceous, from the Red Deer River, Alberta, Canada.

Parasaurolophus walkeri (69)

Parasaurolophus differed from the other hollow crested hadrosaurs in that the nasal passages did not have the complex folding within the crest. The same effect was achieved by simply extending the crest into a long tube. The nasal passages passed to the end of the crest and then returned to the skull and to the internal nostrils. The crest was made up entirely of the premaxillae, the small nasal bones just appearing at the base of the crest above the orbits. When sectioned the crest contained two pairs of tubes, the left and right nasal passages which ran to the end of the crest and thereafter returned.

P. walkeri had a long tubular crest that extended from the duck-bill in a gentle curve that projected beyond the posterior margin of the skull, for a greater distance than the length of the skull itself. In fact the projecting part of the crest was nearly 2m (6½ft) long. This species was the earliest member of the lineage so far recognised; the latest, *P. tubicen*, which was one of the very last of the dinosaurs, had a crest that was even more exaggerated in length. This latter species was from the Ojo Alamo Formation of San Juan County, New Mexico.

P. walkeri comes from the Oldman (Belly River) Formation, Upper Cretaceous, from the Red Deer River, Alberta, Canada.

Parasaurolophus cyrtocristatus (70)

Parasaurolophus cyrtocristatus appeared later than *P. walkeri* but it appears to be more primitive in the development of its crest. Instead of projecting posteriorly in line with the profile of the upper surface of the skull, it bent over towards the back of the neck. This species seems to represent an evolutionary sidebranch from the lineage that culminated in *P. tubicen*.

P. cyrtocristatus comes from the Fruitland Formation, Upper Cretaceous, at Coal Creek, south east of Tsaya, McKinley County (not Coal Creek, north of Tsaya, San Juan County), New Mexico.

Secernosaurus koerneri

Secernosaurus was described in 1979 on the basis of skeletal remains of what was probably a flat-headed hadrosaur. The importance of this form was that it was discovered in South America. Until recently the hadrosaurs were considered to have been completely restricted to North America and Eurasia. The evidence now available indicates that, towards the end of the Cretaceous, a number of dinosaurs that had evolved in North America managed to migrate to South America, where they became established for a short time immediately prior to the final extinction of the dinosaurs.

Secernosaurus comes from the San Jorge Formation, Upper Cretaceous, of Rio Chico, Patagonia, Argentina.

7
Ceratopsia – Horned Dinosaurs

The ceratopsians or horned dinosaurs represented a major group of the ornithischians that evolved during the Upper Cretaceous. Typically this group was characterised by the development of an enormous bony frill from the posterior part of the skull which extended over the neck region and indeed, in some forms, halfway along the back. In some cases the posterior margin of the frill was drawn out into long spikes and in the majority of forms there were median horns on the nasal region of the snout as well as paired horns above and behind the eyes. The early development of the bony frill seems to have been connected with an increase in the length and strength of the jaw muscles. The dentition was formed by a single row of teeth, which had a scissor-like action, the upper and lower rows shearing against one another. It is believed that the ceratopsians, which were among the most successful of the later herbivorous dinosaurs, were particularly well adapted for dealing with exceptionally tough plant materials, such as the tough fronds of palm trees. The snout became very narrow and beak-like and an extra median bone developed at the tip of the upper jaw, the rostral bone, which is the trademark of the ceratopsians as a whole. The elongation of the frill over the back of the neck would have further served as a protection. The most obvious features, the large horns, could also have protected them from the unwelcome attentions of predators.

An analysis in 1975 of the horns and frills has compared these head decorations with similar structures in living reptiles and mammals and has related them to possible patterns of behaviour, such as the establishing of male dominance in the herd as well as display features for the defence of territory. The ceratopsians with merely a small nasal horn were likely to have used this against the flanks of rivals. The forms with long nasal horns probably used them in the same way as living rhinoceroses – although appearing formidable weapons they would have served primarily as threats and would rarely have been used against members of their own species, as they could have caused serious if not fatal damage. The ceratopsians fall into two main groups depending on the types of frill. The short-frilled lineage was characterised by the enlargement of the nasal horns and the small development of the paired. The exception to this is *Triceratops*, the last member of this group, which evolved long paired horns and reduced the nasal horn. In this development *Triceratops* paralleled the condition of the long-frilled ceratopsians, in which the nasal horn remained small and the paired horns were greatly lengthened. It seems probable that these were similar in function to the horns of cattle. As well as their use as weapons against predators they were mainly used in contests between members of the same species. The rival males would lock their horns and push and shove until one of them conceded defeat.

One of the unusual features of the forelimbs of the ceratopsians is that they were not held straight beneath the body as in all the other dinosaurs. Instead they stuck out at an angle, in between that of sprawling reptiles and normal dinosaurs. This means that the width of the trackway made by the two front feet would have been considerably greater than the width of the body. The limbs held in this semi-erect posture would have given the dinosaur much greater stability when engaged in shoving, twisting and generally wrestling with its competitors. One of the functions of the long frills was likely to have been to produce a frontal threat display. It is known that living crocodiles for example are more impressed by increase in the height of rivals or enemies than by width. When for example *Torosaurus* with its 2.6m (8$\frac{1}{2}$ft) long skull lowered its head, the enormous frill would have been raised to frightening heights and effectively intimidated any enemies. The enormous elongated spikes on the posterior edge of the *Styracosaurus* skull would have produced a similar effect although this form was one of the short crested ceratopsians. When the head was lowered, it too would have presented a frightening spectacle.

The ceratopsians were heavily built quadrupeds and represented one of the very few documented examples of a quadrupedal group of dinosaurs descended from a bipedal group. The most primitive, the psittacosaurs or parrot-reptiles which seem to have been able to move as either bipeds or quadrupeds, were formerly classified among the bipedal ornithopods, although it had long been recognised that they possessed a number of ceratopsian characters. The view now held is that the possession of the beginning of a frill along the back of the skull, the incipient nasal horn in some species and the presence of the unique rostral bone are sufficient to include the parrot-reptiles among the ceratopsians. A second primitive family, the protoceratopsians, were characterised by the development of an extensive bony frill. The advanced ceratopsians, the ceratopsids, possessed both enormous frills and long horns with either the single nasal or paired postorbitals being exaggerated at the expense of the others. The ceratopsians appear to have originated in eastern Asia and the protoceratopsians were, in general, confined to Asia apart from one primitive form that flourished in North America at the very end of the Cretaceous.

In North America the most advanced of both short- and long-frilled ceratopsids underwent a major evolutionary radiation.

PSITTACOSAURIDAE

Psittacosaurus mongoliensis (71)

Psittacosaurus, the 'parrot-reptile', was so called because of its sharp downturned upper jaw which gave the impression of the beak of a parrot. There was also the beginnings of a frill developed at the back of the skull. The skeletal feature that enabled *Psittacosaurus* to be classified as a ceratopsian was the existence of the unique rostral bone at the tip of the upper jaw. Although in many respects *Psittacosaurus* appears to be the ideal ancestor of the later ceratopsians the species that have so far been discovered cannot be the actual ancestors because the hands already show a greater reduction of the fingers than in the protoceratopsians and the teeth in the front of the upper jaw have been lost, while they are still present in *Protoceratops*. In spite of these minor differences the overall proportions of *Psittacosaurus* suggest that the ceratopsians evolved from among the psittacosaurids, and ultimately from a hypsilophodont ancestor.

In 1980 the remains of minute specimens of *Psittacosaurus* were described which in life would have had a length of 250mm (10in), and a mass of about 0.7% of the adults. These remains are, to date, among the smallest known dinosaurs and they are important as their teeth already show wear, which means that they were already feeding on fairly tough plant materials. Their minute size, compared with the adults, must have meant that the parents could not have been directly concerned with caring for them, beyond being in the vicinity and protecting the nesting site from predators.

Psittacosaurus comes from Ondai Sair Formation, Lower Cretaceous, of Mongolia. Further species are known from the Lower Cretaceous of Kansu and Shantung, China.

PROTOCERATOPSIDAE

The protoceratopsians show, in differing degrees, the beginnings of the main specialisations of the more advanced ceratopsians. They all had a marked development of the frill and some showed the beginnings of the formation of the single median nasal horn and the paired supraorbital brow horns. Most, however, retained a number of primitive characters such as two teeth in the premaxilla and claws on the fingers and toes, instead of the small hooves that developed in the later larger ceratopsians. The protoceratopsians were a characteristic part of the Upper Cretaceous dinosaur fauna of eastern Asia in Mongolia and China, although one primitive member is known from the end of the Cretaceous in North America.

Leptoceratops gracilis (72)
Leptoceratops is the only protoceratopsian known from North America and was in fact the last representative of this group. The structure of the skull and skeleton was by far the most primitive, except that the two teeth in the premaxilla had been lost. In all other respects *Leptoceratops* appeared to be a survivor of the ancestral type. The frill had developed only slightly and there was no sign of either nasal or brow horn cores. Both the hands and feet bore claws. The foot had only four toes and although there were five fingers on the hand the fourth and fifth were greatly reduced. *Leptoceratops* was a comparatively lightly built form and must have filled an ecological niche different from that of the large heavily built ceratopsians that were its contemporaries.

   Leptoceratops comes from the Upper Edmonton Formation, Upper Cretaceous, from the Red Deer River, Alberta, Canada.

Protoceratops andrewsi (73)
Protoceratops, although only about 2m (6½ft) in length, was a heavily built form which was fully quadrupedal heralding the overall proportions of the large ceratopsians. The most notable feature was the increased extension of the posterior part of the skull, which, apart from the lateral margins, was composed of the most posterior bones of the skull, the parietals. The formation of this frill was directly related to the increase in the length and size of the jaw muscles, which in turn was connected with the development of a powerful shearing dentition to cope with exceptionally tough plant material. The discovery of this dinosaur by the 1924 American Museum of Natural History Expedition to Central Asia (Mongolia) was of particular importance for, not only were there over a hundred skeletons recovered, but all growth stages from hatchling to adult were preserved. Nests of eggs were also discovered by the expedition (Plate VII). The sand had been scooped out to form a shallow depression and then the eggs had been carefully laid in concentric rings before being

buried by the parent. The existence of conspicuous nests and the numerous remains of *Protoceratops* at all stages of growth suggests that the nesting grounds were protected by the adults.

Protoceratops comes from the Djadochta Formation, Santonian, Upper Cretaceous, of Shabarak Usu, Mongolia and also from the Ulan Tsonch Formation, Upper Cretaceous, at Ulan Tsonch, Kansu, China.

Bagaceratops rozhdestvenskyi (74)

Bagaceratops was described in 1975 and was one of the smaller protoceratopsians. It was unusual in that the frill on the back of the skull was only slightly developed, yet already there was a clearly formed horn core. *Bagaceratops* had an unusual mixture of advanced and primitive characters. The premaxilla, for example, was devoid of teeth, which was an advanced feature. Clearly the small squat *Bagaceratops* filled a somewhat different ecological niche from that of *Protoceratops*.

Bagaceratops comes from the Khermeen Tsav Formation, Campanian, Upper Cretaceous, from Khermeen Tsav, Nemegt Basin, Mongolia.

Microceratops gobiensis (75)

Microceratops was the earliest protoceratopsian, appearing in rocks slightly older than those containing *Protoceratops*. Unlike all other ceratopsians *Microceratops* was both very small and slender. In its general proportions it was similar to the hypsilophodonts but with a small frill clearly developed. According to some authors *Microceratops* represented the most primitive of all the ceratopsians and demonstrated its closeness to the likely origin of the group from the hypsilophodonts. The alternative interpretation of *Microceratops* is that it was a specialised side branch that evolved to fill the same type of niche as the small hypsilophodonts in other areas of the world.

Microceratops comes from the Tsondolain Formation, Upper Cretaceous, from Tsondolain Khuduk, Kansu, China and also from the Sheergeen Gashoon Formation, Nemegt Basin, Mongolia.

CERATOPSIDAE

The major evolutionary development of the ceratopsians was confined to North America, although there is some evidence that they reached South America immediately prior to their final extinction. The advanced ceratopsians were all of large size, the largest reaching 9m (30ft) in length. They had three short hooves on the hands and four on the hind feet. The most characteristic feature was the enormous development of the frill at the back of the skull. Although these developed initially as support for the jaw muscles they took on the further function of protection and display. The skulls also developed large horns, a single median nasal horn and a pair of supraorbital or brow horns. There were two major evolutionary lineages – in the short-crested line the nasal horn developed at the expense of the brow horns, whereas in the long-crested line the nasal horn was reduced and the brow horns enormously developed. The one exception to these two trends was in *Triceratops* which was the most advanced of the short-crested lineage. In this case the brow horns increased and the nasal horn was reduced. The other feature in which *Triceratops* differed from all the other ceratopsians was that the frill formed a solid sheet of bone. In all the other forms the frill was perforated by large temporal openings, while in *Triceratops* these had been closed over.

Styracosaurus albertensis (76)
Styracosaurus was a ceratopsian with a most striking appearance. Although a member of the short-crested lineage the posterior margin of the frill bore enormous bony spikes almost equal in length to the main part of the frill itself. This dramatic display structure could hardly have served as a weapon but must have presented a frightening spectacle whenever the head was lowered towards enemies or rivals.

Styracosaurus comes from the Oldman Formation, Upper Cretaceous, from the Red Deer River, Alberta, Canada.

Montanoceratops cerorhynchus (77)
Montanoceratops is structurally one of the most primitive members of the ceratopsid family and some authors consider that it should even be classified as an advanced protoceratopsian. *Montanoceratops* was only 3m (10ft) in length and it still had claws rather than hooves on its fingers and toes. There were still two teeth in the premaxilla but in other respects it was more akin to the advanced ceratopsians. There was a nasal horn developed, the proportions of the body were robust and the forelimbs longer than in the protoceratopsians.

Montanoceratops comes from the St Mary River Formation, Upper Cretaceous, Montana.

Brachyceratops montanensis (78)
Brachyceratops was one of the smallest of the advanced short-crested ceratopsians being only 2.5m (8ft) long. There was, however, a well developed nasal horn core. All the remains of this form that have been found were of immature individuals and it is probable that

Brachyceratops was the juvenile of *Monoclonius*.

Brachyceratops comes from the Two Medicine Formation, Upper Cretaceous, Montana.

Monoclonius nasicornus (79)

Monoclonius bore an enormous nasal horn with mere bumps representing the brow horns. There was a strongly crenulated margin to the back of the frill and a pair of forward directed hooked processes from near the centre of the posterior margin. The possible function of these small projections is as yet unexplained. The first species of *Monoclonius*, *M. crassus*, came from the Judith River Formation of Montana and several other species are known from Montana.

Monoclonius nasicornus comes from the Oldman Formation, Upper Cretaceous, from the Red Deer River, Alberta, Canada.

Pachyrhinosaurus canadensis (80)

Pachyrhinosaurus differs from all other advanced ceratopsians by its very short frill and the absence of either brow or nasal horns. The region of the skull in front of and between the eyes was thickened by a wide mass of bone. This broad flattened boss formed a large prominence and in all probability functioned as a kind of battering ram, which would have been used in contests between rival males. It must have been much less hazardous than the long nasal horn of *Monoclonius*. In many respects *Pachyrhinosaurus* was closely related to *Monoclonius* and there does not seem to be any justification for placing *Pachyrhinosaurus* in a separate family of its own, as some have suggested.

Pachyrhinosaurus comes from the Edmonton Formation, Upper Cretaceous, of Little Bow River Valley and Scabby Butte, Alberta, Canada.

Triceratops horridus (81)

Triceratops was not only the largest of the ceratopsians, reaching a maximum of 9m (30ft) in length, but was one of the most successful dinosaurs of the very end of the Cretaceous. *Triceratops* represented the peak of ceratopsian evolution and marked the end of the short-crested lineage. Its conspicuous success may well have been due to an important change in its behavioural pattern from its short-crested ancestors. The short-crested ceratopsians were characterised by their possession of exceptionally long nasal horns, which must have been used primarily in intimidating displays. It is unlikely that they would have been used as weapons among members of the same species, as they would have caused extremely serious damage. The reduction of the nasal horn with the concomitant increase in the length of the brow horns suggests that the intraspecific contests of *Triceratops* involved the locking of the brow horns in the manner of cattle and then shoving and pushing until one individual conceded defeat and retreated. The bony crest of *Triceratops* was further distinguished from all the other ceratopsians in that it formed a solid sheet of bone, the normal large perforation having become secondarily closed. There is no doubt that such struggles between individuals of the same species actually did take place, because many of the frills bear scars, where they had been scored by the horns of fellow *Triceratops*.

Triceratops comes from the Lance Formation, Upper Cretaceous, of Wyoming, as well as from Colorado, Montana, Alberta and Saskatchewan.

Chasmosaurus belli (82)
Chasmosaurus was the most primitive member of the long-crested lineage. The crest was more than twice the normal length of the skull and formed a large triangle with the apex at the snout and the posterior edge forming a straight margin with sharp wide angles. The lateral edge was crenulated. When the head was lowered this huge triangle would have been raised to present a huge expanse, which would have served to intimidate potential foes or rivals. The forward projecting brow horns would have locked with those of individuals of the same species for trials of strength to establish supremacy, whenever the visual display alone did not serve. This dinosaur was originally included in *Monoclonius* in 1902 but in 1914 was transferred to *Protorosaurus*. However this name had already been established for a Permian lizard-like reptile as far back as 1830 and so the name was replaced by *Chasmosaurus*.

Chasmosaurus comes from the Oldman (Belly River) Formation, Upper Cretaceous, from the Red Deer River, Alberta, Canada.

Arrhinoceratops brachyops (83)
Arrhinoceratops was characterised by the reduction of the nasal horn and the increase in the forward facing brow horns. The lateral margin of the frill was closely crenulated with small triangular bony plates. Although *Arrhinoceratops* was a close relative of *Chasmosaurus* the outline of the frill did not exhibit the striking triangular shape.

Arrhinoceratops comes from the Edmonton Formation, Upper Cretaceous, from the Red Deer River, Alberta, Canada and also from the North Horn Formation, Utah.

Anchiceratops ornatus (84)

Anchiceratops was a near relation of *Arrhinoceratops* and had prominent forward facing brow horns and a greatly reduced nasal horn. The characteristic feature of *Anchiceratops* was the formation of rounded knob-like protuberances towards the posterior end of the median longitudinal ridge of the frill.

Anchiceratops comes from the Lower Edmonton Formation, Upper Cretaceous, from the Red Deer River, Alberta, Canada.

Pentaceratops sternbergii (85)

Pentaceratops was so named because its skull appeared to have five horns. There were two long brow horns together with a moderately sized nasal horn and, above the angle of the jaw, the jugal bone projected out sideways forming a sharp lateral spike giving the impression of an extra pair of horns, hence the name.

Pentaceratops comes from the Fruitland Beds Formation, Upper Cretaceous, New Mexico.

Torosaurus latus (86)

Torosaurus marks the culmination of the long-crested line. The largest skull of this dinosaur measured 2.6m ($8\frac{1}{2}$ft) from the tip of the snout to the back of the frill, making it the largest skull of any land animal known. The brow horns were massive and, unlike all its predecessors, the lateral margins of the frill were smooth with no sign of any crenulations or other types of ornament. The end of the Cretaceous was dominated by *Triceratops* but prior to the final extinction of the dinosaurs most of the *Triceratops* had died out. However, *Torosaurus* survived till the very end as one of the very last surviving dinosaurs.

Torosaurus comes from the Lance Formation, Upper Cretaceous, of Niobrara County, Wyoming.

8
Ankylosauria – Fused Dinosaurs

The ankylosaurs were one of the major divisions of the ornithischians that show no evidence of ever having passed through a bipedal stage in their evolution. Without exception they were quadrupedal and were characterised by the retention of primitive bony scutes in the skin. These small bony dermal or skin plates occurred in the most primitive saurischian *Ornithosuchus* and in the lightly built primitive ornithopod *Hypsilophodon* and were the normal feature of the thecodonts, which gave rise to the dinosaurs. Hence it is not surprising that the earliest and most primitive dinosaurs tended to possess them. The major feature of the ankylosaurs is that, not only did they keep this primitive bony armour, but they developed it to such an extreme degree that in the advanced types it formed a solid carapace fused to the underlying ribs, vertebrae and pelvic girdle. The development of the heavy armour was also reflected in the change in proportions of the body, which became broader with short legs. There is evidence that the limbs were often held in the squat sprawling posture of primitive reptiles, although this seems to have been acquired secondarily from the more primitive slender upright forms. This secondary acquisition of a primitive posture also resulted in the articulating surface of the limb girdle becoming a solid sheet of bone and not open as in all other dinosaurs. This seemingly primitive feature was a secondary redevelopment and not the retention of a primitive condition. The neck also became shorter and the bony plates became fused to the skull, completely obliterating the normal perforations which characterised all the other dinosaurs. The skull was by far the most advanced of any dinosaur in the development of a complete bony secondary palate, separating the food and air passages, in exactly the same way as in mammals.

In view of the massive nature of the bony armour which makes the ankylosaurs ideal forms for being preserved as fossils it is noteworthy that their remains are amongst the rarest of the dinosaurs. From their proportions and massive weight, they were unlikely to have inhabited lowland marshy areas where many of the other dinosaurs flourished and it seems that they must have lived in regions where little sediment was being deposited. The few complete remains that have been found have invariably been preserved lying upside down. It is unlikely that any predator could have actively turned a 3 or 4 tonne ankylosaur onto its back. These occurrences probably represented individuals whose bodies were washed downstream by rivers and, as they rotted, the gases produced would have turned them over so that when the gases broke through or the carcase was beached on a sand bank it would have been upside down. The ankylosaurs fall into three groups – an ancestral family represented by *Scelidosaurus*, a further primitive family, the acanthopholids, and the advanced nodosaurs.

SCELIDOSAURIDAE

Scelidosaurus harrisoni (87)

Scelidosaurus was one of the most primitive of all the ornithischians, being closer in its structure to the semiaquatic armoured quadrupedal ancestors of the dinosaurs than perhaps any other dinosaur. This suggests that the ornithischians evolved from two closely related lines of herbivorous thecodont reptiles. *Scelidosaurus* became a land dwelling herbivore before the difference in the relative lengths of the fore and hind limbs had become so exaggerated that the easiest means of locomotion was on two feet. The retention of a comparatively slow method of walking and its obvious disadvantages as far as encounters with flesh-eaters were concerned were to a large extent compensated for by the increased development of the bony armour. *Scelidosaurus* had longitudinal rows of keeled scutes, which formed short pointed spikes running along the length of the back, and there were additional longitudinal rows of elongated scutes running the length of the body. For a long time *Scelidosaurus* was considered to be the ancestor of the stegosaurs which similarly had a double row of upstanding bony plates running the length of the body. The fact that *Scelidosaurus* came from the Lower Jurassic and *Stegosaurus* from the Upper Jurassic, whilst the ankylosaurs were known from the succeeding Cretaceous period provided strong circumstantial evidence that *Scelidosaurus* was a primitive stegosaur. However, in its general proportions and the type of armour, it was also very similar to the primitive ankylosaurs. In general *Scelidosaurus* has been placed close to the common ancestry of both ankylosaurs and stegosaurs. A newly discovered skeleton of a juvenile specimen that is as yet still undescribed but which has been extracted from a limestone boulder by the use of acetic acid by A. E. Rixon of the British Museum (Natural

History), London, has partly resolved the question. The pelvic girdle does not have a prepubic process and in this respect differs from the stegosaurs and is similar to the ankylosaurs. However, from the discovery of a similar type of pelvic girdle in *Lesothosaurus* and *Heterodontosaurus*, the two most primitive ornithopod ornithischians, this type of pelvic girdle was the basic ornithischian pattern. Since the ankylosaurs have retained this, it is probably more appropriate to classify *Scelidosaurus* as the most primitive of the ankylosaurs. A third specimen, the back of the skull and spike-bearing neck, was discovered in 1980 and prepared by R. A. Langham.

Scelidosaurus comes from the Lower Liassic, Lower Jurassic of Charmouth, Lyme Regis, Dorset, England.

ACANTHOPHOLIDAE

The acanthopholids include the least specialised of the typical ankylosaurs. Their bodies were of more normal reptilian proportions, having a fairly high and narrow trunk, and the necks were comparatively long. There tended to be strong vertical spines developed on the back over the shoulders and along the neck, which would have provided protection for this vulnerable region. In the hip or pelvic region there was a tendency for the plates of the dermal armour to fuse together into large bony blankets or bucklers but these were not fused to the underlying bones of the skeleton.

Acanthopholis horridus (88)

Acanthopholis was one of the least specialised of all the ankylosaurs and in many respects was not significantly different from *Scelidosaurus*. There was a double row of triangular spikes situated along the dorsal side of the neck and shoulder region. The rest of the trunk was armoured with raised oval plates embedded in the skin, forming longitudinal rows running the length of the body and tail.

Acanthopholis comes from the Lower Chalk, Upper Cretaceous, of Folkestone, Kent, England.

Struthiosaurus transylvanicus (89)

Struthiosaurus was described originally in 1871 from the Gosau Formation of the Turonian (Upper Cretaceous) of Austria, and in 1915 F. von Nopcsa described further material, which he identified as also belonging to *Struthiosaurus*. This ankylosaur was one of the last surviving dinosaurs and the last primitive acanthopholid ankylosaur. It was one of the smallest ankylosaurs and its armour consisted of small oval plates embedded in the skin, with a few pairs of spines protecting the neck.

Struthiosaurus comes from the Maestrichtian, Upper Cretaceous, of Romania.

Polacanthus foxi (90)

Polacanthus is sometimes classified with the advanced ankylosaurs and at other times with the primitive ones. However, as it does not seem to have developed the typical specialisations of the advanced forms, it is here retained as a specialised example of the acanthopholids. The basic pattern of the armour can be directly compared with that of *Acanthopholis* and even *Scelidosaurus*. The neck and shoulder regions were protected by a row of large laterally directed spines. On the tail there were sharp flat vertical bony plates. Most of the rest of the armour comprised small oval plates embedded in the skin. However, in the region of pelvic girdle the armour was fused into a wide rectangular bony blanket or buckler. This development in many ways heralds the solid armour of the advanced ankylosaurs but differed from them in that it was not fused to any part of the underlying skeleton.

   Polacanthus comes from the Wealden Beds, Lower Cretaceous, of the Isle of Wight, England.

Hylaeosaurus armatus

Hylaeosaurus armatus was described from a block of Wealden sandstone from Cuckfield in Sussex by Gideon Mantell in 1833 and was included by Owen among the first group of reptiles which he recognised as dinosaurs. Later in 1844 Mantell proposed that *Hylaeosaurus* should be named *H. oweni* as he felt that this was more appropriate. Unfortunately the supposed inappropriateness of a name is not a valid reason to change it and so *H. armatus* must stand. Under the direction of Owen a life-sized model of *Hylaeosaurus* was constructed but unfortunately there is still insufficient evidence on which to describe *Hylaeosaurus*, beyond the fact that it was an ankylosaur.

Silvisaurus condrayi (91)

Silvisaurus shows a number of features similar to those of *Polacanthus*. A large area above the pelvic region is fused into a bony buckler and there were sharp spines projecting laterally in the shoulder region as well as a series on the tail behind the sacral buckler. From behind the head up to the buckler were rows of thick rectangular bony plates similar to those of such an advanced form as *Ankylosaurus* itself and it seems likely that *Silvisaurus* may well have been ancestral to the advanced forms.

Silvisaurus comes from the Dakota Formation, Upper Cretaceous, of Kansas.

NODOSAURIDAE (ANKYLOSAURIDAE)

The nodosaurs were characterised by their broad and flattened bodies with short necks. The bony armour tended to be massively developed and was fused to the underlying parts of the skeleton such as the ribs, vertebrae and pelvic girdle. The pelvic girdle was not open at the articulation but had been secondarily closed by bone. The pubis which had a forward prepubic process in the more primitive acanthopholids had lost it and the entire pubis was reduced to a tiny nubbin of bone. The skull also showed remarkable changes in that bony dermal elements covered the normal skull-pattern obscuring all the details and making the skulls hardly recognisable as belonging to dinosaurs.

Panoplosaurus mirus (92)

Panoplosaurus was described from a complete skull and parts of a skeleton. This form was one of the most advanced ankylosaurs and illustrates dramatically the way in which the fusion of the bony head armour to the underlying skull has completely obliterated the normal reptilian skull pattern. Only the nostrils and orbits penetrate this protective bony thickening.

Panoplosaurus comes from the Oldman Formation, Upper Cretaceous, from the Red Deer River, Alberta, Canada.

Ankylosaurus magniventris (93)

Ankylosaurus is the typical example of the advanced ankylosaurs and has given its name to the entire group. The skull was short and had short triangular spines at its posterior corners which gave the false impression of ears. The dermal armour was fused to the skull and behind the head there was a series of rows of massive rectangular raised plates, which ran the entire length of the body, down to the tip of the tail which ended in a rounded bilobed club.

Although *Ankylosaurus* is one of the best known of the ankylosaurs its name has been a source of great confusion. In 1902 an armoured dinosaur was described from the Oldman Formation of Alberta under the name *Stereocephalus*. The author then discovered that the name had already been used for another animal so in 1910 he replaced it with the name *Euoplocephalus*. However, in the meantime in 1908, another specimen had been described under the name *Ankylosaurus* and so, as all these dinosaurs were considered to be the same, the first valid name to be used was *Ankylosaurus* and so this must be the correct one. A recent author has suggested that the two specimens were not the same and so both names can still be used. In any case *Ankylosaurus magniventris* is the correct name for the skeleton on which the present restoration has been based.

Ankylosaurus comes from the Hell Creek Beds, Upper Cretaceous, of Montana.

Scolosaurus cutleri (94)

Scolosaurus was based on a well preserved skeleton which is on display in the British Museum (Natural History), London. The armour comprised a series of bands, each of which carried six large spines, which continued to the end of the tail, although beyond the pelvic region their number was reduced. The tip of the tail itself ended in a club-like lump, which bore two large vertical spines side by side.

Scolosaurus comes from the Oldman Formation, Upper Cretaceous, from the Red Deer River, Alberta, Canada.

Palaeoscincus rugosidens (95)

Palaeoscincus costatus was described by Leidy in 1856 on the basis of a few ridged teeth from the Judith River Formation of Montana. When the partial skeleton with its armour of rectangular ridged plates, together with large sharp spines projecting laterally along the margin of the carapace, was discovered, it was assigned to *Palaeoscincus* but placed in a new species *P. rugosidens* as its teeth differed somewhat from Leidy's original discovery. In the meantime, remains of a similar dinosaur from the Edmonton Formation of Alberta had been named *Edmontonia* and it has been suggested that *P. rugosidens* should be included in *Edmontonia*. However, it seems preferable to retain the name *Palaeoscincus* for the present.

Palaeoscincus comes from the Two Medicine Formation, Upper Cretaceous, of Montana.

Nodosaurus textilis (96)

The advanced ankylosaurs are placed in the family Nodosauridae as this family name was given before that of the Ankylosauridae and was based on the original description of *Nodosaurus*. The armour consisted of a pavement of small plates arranged in transverse rows down the body. Over the ribs were lines of small rectangular plates and between these rows, and situated between the ribs, were larger plates each bearing a rounded bony node, hence the name. The bony plates that were situated just beneath the skin had surface markings similar to that of textile hence the second name.

Nodosaurus comes from the Upper Cretaceous of Benton, Wyoming.

Saichania chulsanensis (IV)

Saichania is based on a complete skull associated with the anterior part of the armoured carapace. The heavy bony armour covered the skull and at the lateral edges of the carapace there were strong triangular spikes. The bones of the skull, including the quadrate, were fused to one another and one of the curious features was the presence of an accessory nasal opening. This was in all probability connected with the opening of the salt gland. This specimen with its massive forelimbs is beautifully preserved and was, in fact, named from the Mongolian word for beautiful – *saichan*.

Saichania comes from the Barum Goyot Formation of the Upper Cretaceous of Khulsan, Nemegt Basin, Mongolia.

9
Stegosauria – Roofed Dinosaurs

STEGOSAURIDAE

The stegosaurs or roofed dinosaurs are the fourth major group of the ornithischian dinosaurs and one of the most impressive looking. All the stegosaurs were characterised by two rows of flat plates or spines running along the dorsal surface of the back from just behind the skull down to the end of the tail. The skull was long and narrow, the dentition was feeble although there were characteristic ornithischian cheek pouches. The body was narrow and high in the pelvic region, where the largest spines or plates were carried. Although the forelimbs were very much shorter than the hind there is no evidence that they were derived from bipedal ancestors. In fact the primitive armoured *Scelidosaurus* was for a long time classified as the most primitive of the stegosaurs and although it is now included among the ankylosaurs, it is likely that the stegosaurs originated from a scelidosaur. The feature which distinguishes the stegosaurs is the strong development of the prepubic process of the pelvic girdle and the specialisation of the armour to form the impressive paired rows of plates and spines along the back. This armour was embedded in the skin and was not directly connected to the underlying skeleton.

The earliest stegosaurs proper are found in England and they achieved their major success during the Upper Jurassic in Europe, Asia and Africa. Fragmentary remains are claimed to be present in the Upper Cretaceous of India.

Tuojiangosaurus multispinus (97)

Tuojiangosaurus was described in 1977 from China and was based on a nearly complete skeleton. From just behind the skull to half way along the tail were fifteen pairs of triangular plates with those positioned above the pelvic region elongated to produce spike-like structures. *Tuojiangosaurus* is one of the three adequately known stegosaurs and is of particular importance as it seems to represent the basic stegosaur pattern from which can be derived the more specialised African and American forms.

From the condition illustrated by *Tuojiangosaurus* with its fifteen pairs of plates, there seem to have been developments in two directions, both involving a reduction in the number of paired structures. One development was towards accentuating the triangular plates and the other was towards developing longer and sharper spines.

Tuojiangosaurus comes from the Upper Jurassic of Zigong 240km (150 miles) north west of Chungking, Szechuan, China.

Chialingosaurus kuani
The first important stegosaur remains to be described from China came from the Upper Jurassic of Taipingtsai, Pinganhsiang, 200km (125 miles) north of Chungking, Szechuan, and were referred to *Chialingosaurus* and compared with the African *Kentrosaurus*. It was not possible to produce a detailed restoration from the remains and future research may well show that this form belongs to *Tuojiangosaurus*. If this should be the case the name *Chialingosaurus* will have to be used for both.

Kentrosaurus aethiopicus (98)
One of the important discoveries made during the German excavations at Tendaguru in 1909–1912 was of numerous remains of a stegosaur, which enabled a complete reconstruction of the skeleton to be mounted. This is on display in the Palaeontological Museum of Humboldt University, Berlin. Small triangular bony plates were present in the neck and shoulder region but in the middle of the back and especially over the pelvic region these become long sharp pointed spines with one immediately above the hind leg projecting sideways. The pair of spikes at the end of the tail, which was a characteristic feature of all the stegosaurs, appeared in *Kentrosaurus* to be placed at the very tip.

The name *Kentrosaurus* was erected by Hennig in 1915 but it was pointed out that an American dinosaur had already been named *Centrosaurus*, and so in 1916 Hennig proposed the new name *Kentrurosaurus* and Nopcsa the name *Doryphorosaurus* as replacements. In fact these two new names were entirely redundant. The name *Kentrosaurus* was perfectly valid and remains so to this day.

Kentrosaurus comes from the Upper Jurassic of Tendaguru, Tanzania.

Stegosaurus armatus (99)
Stegosaurus was the largest known stegosaur reaching a length of 9m (30ft). The end of the tail was equipped with two pairs of sharp spikes but the most notable features of this dinosaur were the enormous triangular bony plates along the dorsal part of the back. The largest

was positioned at the highest part of the body above the pelvic girdle. As these plates were embedded in the skin there is no certain way of determining the angle at which they were orientated, and some authors have placed them flat with the points facing laterally. In fact, the traditional vertical orientation is probably the one that is true to life, since this would produce the least strain on the skin in which they were embedded.

In most restorations the arrangement of the plates is shown as staggered or alternate, in contrast to the arrangement of the armour of all other armoured reptiles, both dinosaur and non-dinosaur. Recently in 1976 this supposed alternate arrangement of the plates was explained as functioning as 'convective heat loss fins', a special mechanism for getting rid of excess heat. This interpretation was supported by a series of wind tunnel experiments and the comparison of the structure of manufactured convective heat loss fins which are purposely designed in a staggered arrangement. Unfortunately there is no evidence that *Stegosaurus* plates were arranged alternately. This idea was based on the position of the plates found in association with a complete skeleton. The skeleton was lying on its side and the plates, having been originally embedded in skin, simply fell down when this disintegrated. It would not have been possible for them to have fallen exactly on top of one another, so they would have given an accidental impression of being staggered when the remains were first excavated.

There is one other feature of the anatomy of *Stegosaurus* for which it has become famous and that is the supposed existence of a huge nerve ganglion in the sacrum which was many times larger than the brain. This has given rise to the popular notion of *Stegosaurus* having a 'second brain'. Unfortunately there is no evidence that the large cavity in the canal for the spinal cord actually housed an enormous nerve ganglion. It is much more likely that in this place there was a glycogen gland, which acted as a kind of energy booster for the hind limbs, exactly as occurs in modern birds.

Nevertheless, there is no doubt that *Stegosaurus* was a sensational looking dinosaur that richly deserves the popularity it has gained. It died out halfway through the Age of Dinosaurs.

Stegosaurus comes from the Morrison Formation, Upper Jurassic, of Colorado.

10
The Extinction of the Dinosaurs

Perhaps one of the greatest mysteries in the history of life on Earth was the sudden extinction of the dinosaurs. Surprisingly it is not at all difficult to work out theories to account for their demise. Indeed this particular topic is one of the most popular areas for unbridled speculation. The innumerable theories fall into two broad categories: in one group it is considered that the solution can be sought by studying Earthly events which may have taken place over hundreds of thousands of years – a gradualist Earth model; the second group attributes the extinction to a sudden catastrophic extraterrestrial event. In both sets of theories there is a tendency for an expert in one narrow area of science to apply his own specialised knowledge to the problem and to claim that data in his own field provides the solution. Most theories of this kind fail because their authors tend to be ignorant of relevant data in other disciplines. There are certain basic facts that have to be accounted for in any theory of the extinction of the dinosaurs. From a study of the sediments in which dinosaur remains are preserved, it is clear that the final extinction of the dinosaurs was a sudden event in geological terms, which means that it could in fact have extended over hundreds of thousands of years. Now it is known that other reptiles of the time, such as the dolphin-like ichthyosaurs, the barrel-shaped four paddled plesiosaurs and the sea-serpent-like marine lizards, the mosasaurs, also died out at the same time, as did the so-called 'flying reptiles', the warm-blooded furry pterosaurs. Furthermore the ammonites, shelled relatives of the cuttlefish, died out, as did the majority of species of microscopic organisms inhabiting the surface waters of the oceans. It is surely stretching credulity too far to imagine that this virtual simultaneous extinction of what has been calculated as 75% of living species could have been simply coincidence. It seems perfectly reasonable to suggest that these extinctions were likely to have been related to the same general causes. It is however not good enough to propose a comprehensive theory that would explain these extinctions across the board. It is equally necessary to be able to explain the survival of those groups that seemed not to have been affected by the drama going on around them. The small mammals together with the birds seemed to have flourished during this period of crisis and even among the reptiles lizards and snakes, turtles and crocodiles seem to have been singularly unaffected. Insect and plant life on the land and cuttlefish and advanced bony fishes in the oceans seem not to have been adversely affected. Any theory to be viable has to provide some kind of explanation by postulating some cause that selectively attacks the large animals on the land and the microscopic organisms in the surface waters of the oceans. On the land, plant and insect life, birds, mammals and reptiles (apart from dinosaurs and pterosaurs) were unaffected. The basic ecosystem on land was not adversely affected. The large herbivores and the carnivores which preyed upon them, always the more vulnerable and expendable parts of the food web, succumbed. In the oceans it was a very different matter. The base of the food chain, the microscopic plants of the surface waters, suffered a catastrophic extinction and the effects of this were spread throughout the entire ecosystem. Although the plankton recovered this was not in time to save the ammonites and the marine reptiles; only the more adaptable and efficient cuttlefish and teleost bony fish managed. The answer to the problem of extinction must be sought in a phenomenon that would affect the base of a marine food chain and the summit of a terrestrial one. There is some evidence that the extinction on the land may not have been simultaneous with that in the seas, that the land extinctions may have lagged behind by anything up to 500,000 years. If this suggestion is confirmed then this time lag has also to be explained in the context of the overall crisis that affected life on Earth.

Having outlined the basic background information which must be accomodated in any overall theory of dinosaur extinction, it is now possible to examine critically some of the current theories being advocated to account for the end of the dinosaurs. The most exciting theories are those that invoke extraterrestrial agents. The recent discovery of a thin layer of clay at the end of the Age of Dinosaurs which contains 20 times the amount of iridium than is usually found on the Earth has given a tremendous impetus to theories of cosmic catastrophes. This rare element is commonly found in meteorites and the asteroids and it has been calculated that, for such an amount of iridium to be present, it must have come from an extraterrestrial source and that an asteroid some 10 to 20km (6 to 12 miles) in diameter must have struck the Earth. The scenario that is proposed is that on impact such a mass of particles would have thrown up into the atmosphere that the sunlight would have been obliterated and that plant life would in consequence have been unable to photosynthesise. According to this theory green plants of the oceans and continents perished and the animals that fed on the plants similarly succumbed so that food chains both on land and sea collapsed. Only small animals subsisting on seeds and roots and scavenging the rotting remains of this catastrophe of truly biblical proportions were able to hang on until the skies cleared several years later and life on Earth could pull itself together again. The discovery of this iridium rich deposit has at least put paid to the previously popular notion that radiation from a nearby super nova explosion brought the curtain down on the dinosaurs. The asteroid or giant meteor explanation has the great popular appeal of high drama and curiously coincided with the release of a 'disaster' film on the same theme! Such theories are certainly an advance on invoking the wrath of a Deity but not very much.

The real trouble with this category of theory, in which dinosaurs left the stage with a bang, is that it is almost impossible with such a scenario to explain the reason why so many other groups seemed not to have been aware of the great global commotion that was supposedly enveloping them.

The latest variation on this theme is that a comet struck the earth and that the dinosaurs died out as a consequence of the atmospheric heating. The marine phytoplankton is then supposed to have perished as a consequence of the poisoning by cyanide released into the atmosphere by the comet. At least this hypothesis recognised the necessity of providing an explanation to wipe out giant land animals together with microscopic surface dwelling marine organisms.

The other brand of theory involves a careful consideration of all the evidence that can be accumulated, drawing both from biology and geology. These more synthetic theories tend to be less exciting but are more likely to approximate to what actually occurred. They are not as popular as the cosmic cataclysms but are able to encompass more evidence. From studies of living reptiles, it has been shown that for example in giant land tortoises the heat produced by the normal metabolic processes is matched by evaporative heat loss at 24°C but above this it is necessary for there to be additional cooling mechanisms. In fact for large reptiles increased heat is perhaps the one environmental change with which they were least able to cope.

Towards the end of the Cretaceous period there is clear evidence from carbon and oxygen isotope studies that there was a marked increase in temperature. From the microscopic study of the structure

The moist subtropical forests of Montana immediately prior to the extinction of the dinosaurs (from L. Van Valen and R. E. Sloan).

of dinosaur eggshells, it is evident that they were suffering from some kind of stress, if experience with laying birds is anything to go by. The inference is that this may have been heat stress, which would have adversely affected their reproduction cycle. There is evidence of increased temperature but the question arises as to the possible reason for this. A recent suggestion relates this to the geographical changes that took place at the end of the Cretaceous. The Earth was characterised by extensive lowlands and shallow seas and with the retreat of the seas that took place at the end of the Cretaceous the area of marine conditions was significantly reduced so that the consumption of carbon dioxide by marine plants was reduced. The increase in carbon dioxide would have led to the 'runaway greenhouse effect' in which excess heat from the Earth's surface could not have escaped into space through the carbon dioxide thus producing a global temperature rise, which would have adversely affected the microplankton as well as the large terrestrial animals – the dinosaurs. An increase in the temperature of the surface waters of the oceans would have reduced the fertility of the waters simply because this reduces the amount of oxygen that can be held in solution. Following the sharp temperature rise there was then a gradual and continuing reduction in temperature and it was probably this that was the final straw for the dinosaurs. To date there has been only one detailed analysis of what actually happened at the very end of the Age of Dinosaurs. This was done in Montana in the United States, where the gradual replacement of conditions of subtropical forests by open woodland dominated by pines has been documented. As the woodland environment gradually spread southwards so too did the different faunas. The dominant animals of the subtropical forests were duck-billed dinosaurs and ceratopsians together with bone-headed dinosaurs, clawed dinosaurs, ostrich dinosaurs and tyrannosaurs. There were also lizards and snakes as well as a number of mammals, including marsupial possums, insectivores and the rodent-like multituberculates. As open woodland spread, so too did the fauna dominated by mammals. The commonest forms were the herbivorous condylarths (which later gave rise to all the major groups of herbivorous mammals), the first primates made their appearance, and the multituberculates and insectivores were still in evidence.

Where this mammalian fauna appeared it was by far the more dominant; the dinosaur fauna was reduced to about a twentieth of its original strength. The ceratopsians for example were reduced to a tenth of their former numbers. The evidence from this detailed study clearly documents an example of gradual ecological replacement of the dinosaurs by the mammals. Although direct competition between small plant-eating mammals and giant herbivorous dinosaurs does not seem likely at first sight, when it is realised that a single 3 tonne hadrosaur is equivalent in terms of biomass to 10,000 rat sized mammals, it is not too difficult to accept that in competition for food resources a plague of mammals would have the advantage over a few large dinosaurs.

The temperate woodland of Montana at the time of the extinction of the dinosaurs and their replacement by mammals (from L. Van Valen and R. E. Sloan).

In a geological perspective the extinction of the dinosaurs was a sudden event, but in terms of the generations of individuals it would have appeared at the time to have been a slow gradual decline, lasting anything up to 500,000 years. The combination of climatic changes and mammalian competition in the changing conditions seems to be the most acceptable theory to account for the extinction of the dinosaurs. As new evidence comes to hand, it is certainly possible that this synthetic view will have to be modified.

The passing of the dinosaurs was important in one respect. It enabled the descendants of the paramammals to fill all the newly available ecological niches and the Age of Mammals was able to dawn culminating in the evolution of man. In one sense, just as the paramammals did not perish without issue but gave rise to the true mammals, such also was the experience of the dinosaurs, they too did not vanish without issue: their direct descendants are still with us, invested in feathers, as birds.

Appendix
A Note on Dinosaur Colour

The first colour illustration is of the duck-billed dinosaur *Tsintaosaurus* which has a striking colour pattern; indeed throughout the colour section there is a considerable range of both colouring and pattern. There is no way in which the exact colours of dinosaur skin could ever be determined but, from our knowledge of the animal world today, it seems highly unlikely that the dinosaurs were simply a monotonous dull grey or brown. It is necessary to postulate that they would have been coloured in a variety of ways.

The colour patterns that have been given to the dinosaurs in this book are based on an analysis of patterns found among living reptiles and also large living mammals, taken in conjunction with the environments in which they lived and their general way of life. The most primitive dinosaurs were the carnivorous carnosaurs and coelurosaurs which evolved from semiaquatic crocodile-like predators. In this instance it seems reasonable to postulate that the basic type of colouring would have been similar to that found among living crocodiles. The underside is generally light and yellowish but at the sides and over the back there is a mottled pattern of discrete patches of black, browns and yellows. As these reptiles grow larger the patterning becomes less conspicuous although the under surface remains lighter. The carnosaurs and coelurosaurs have been given a mottled patterning mainly of different shades of browns with subsidiary blacks, yellows and white. The smaller forms have the brightest colouring and most prominent patterning. With the advanced carnivores such as the deinonychosaurs, which were leaping dinosaurs, the basic mottling has been modified to give an appearance reminiscent of the big cats, since they filled a comparable ecological niche. Similarly the ornithomimosaurs or ostrich dinosaurs have been given large broken patterns of a combination of browns, black and white. The forms inhabiting wooded areas have a more broken pattern that serves as camouflage, whereas those inhabiting open country have the emphasis on strong blocks of black and white to break up the outline of the body, in much the same way as does the black and white plumage of the ostrich.

The prosauropods and sauropods which came from a stock close to the coelurosaurs have the same basic colours still but in broader bands. Being herbivores they would have had protective coloration with the light underbelly acting as countershading so that, with shadowing, the overall tones of the body would be the same and not stand out prominently (as on a white shadowless background). As these quadrupedal dinosaurs became larger the patterning became less obvious until the skin had a simple monochrome of greys or browns, in much the same way that elephants and rhinoceroses do at the present day. The only major change was that, as these dinosaurs became progressively larger and hence larger expanses of their skins were exposed to direct sunlight, it is likely that as a protective measure against ultra violet rays the larger ones would have darker shades of grey.

The ornithischian dinosaurs were exclusively plant-eating and the smaller forms are likely to have inhabited dense undergrowth. Comparing them with forest dwelling lizards, it seems probable that they would have had strong patterns of greens, browns, yellows and black acting as effective camouflage. Partly to emphasise their herbivorous nature, the ornithischians have been given colour patterns in which green is prominent. As the size of the dinosaurs increased the patterning would have formed larger patches and been less evident. Forms that inhabited dark cypress swamps would have reflected this type of habitat with black and dark greens predominating; forms living in broadleaf woodlands would have tended to have a combination of large patches of browns, greens and yellows, as for example in *Tsintaosaurus*; while forms living in open shrubland would have had the browns predominating. The ceratopsians which evolved from small bipedal herbivores probably had the same basic colouring of greens with subsidiary browns. Again as these increased in size, the patterning became less conspicuous until the largest forms had a uniform grey-green tone.

The armoured dinosaurs, the ankylosaurs, were among the most primitive of the dinosaurs, which had not developed very far from their primitive semiaquatic ancestors. Their likely colouring would have been reminiscent of living crocodiles but again, as basically herbivorous animals, it is likely that there was a green component in their overall brown colouring. The later fully terrestrial forms are likely to have been brown or grey as would have been the case with their descendants, the stegosaurs.

Index

Figures in italics refer to page numbers of illustrations; those in **bold** refer to colour plates.

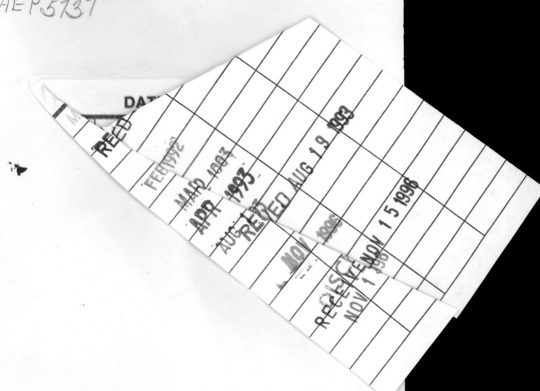